Distance Education in India

Published by
Saurabh Publishing House

Distance Education in India

Yogesh Rana

Saurabh
Publishing House
4735/22, Prakash Deep Building,
Ansari Road, Daryaganj,
New Delhi - 110002

Published by
SAURABH PUBLISHING HOUSE

Distributed by:
Lotus Press Publishers & Distributors
Unit No. 220, Second Floor, 4735/22, Prakash Deep Building,
Ansari Road, Darya Ganj, New Delhi-110002
Ph: 23280047, 32903912, 098118-38000
E-mail : loutspress1984@gmail.com
www.lotuspress.co.in

Saurabh Publishing House is an imprint of
Lotus Press Publishers & Distributors

Distance Education in India

ISBN : 978-81-89005-68-9 (PB)

Printed at : **Lotus Press Publishers & Distributors, New Delhi**

Preface

With education increasingly becoming the primary determinant of overall development in the emerging knowledge economy, the very modes of education have undergone a sea-change, and education in India through distance-learning has reached a crucial stage in its implementation. Having already made great inroads and taken strides in becoming an important part of the educational process in the country, distance education has arrived at the point where the focus has shifted from its implementation to issues of quality control and greater recognition of the degrees it awards to students.

The present text has been designed as a manual which looks into what entails distance education in India. The book makes an assessment of what it means avail of the distance education services available in India, how the process got implemented in the first place, and how distance education is shaping up to become the next great phase in the journey of Indian education. Focus has also been concentrated upon the challenges and issues that still belie distance education in India, and the book also incorporates evaluation of the various developmental programmes undertaken by the government regarding distance education in both urban as well as rural areas.

It is hoped that the incisive and comprehensive content proves highly useful for all. Any suggestions for further improvement are most welcome.

Author

CONTENTS

1

Distance Education System

Distance education is any educational process in which all or most of the teaching is conducted by someone removed in space and/or time from the learner, with the effect that all or most of the communication between teachers and learners is through an artificial medium, either electronic or print. By definition, in distance education the normal or principal means of communication is through technology. Obviously teachers in conventional classrooms may use technology as a supplement to their teaching, but since it is not their principal means of communication the classroom is not considered to be distance education. Another way of discriminating between distance and other forms of education is to ask where the principal educational decisions are made. Who is deciding. what is to be learned? When and how is it to be learned? When has learning been satisfactorily completed? If such decisions are made in the classroom, this is not distance education. If they are made elsewhere and communicated by a technology that is called distance education.

The "open" nature of education that is mediated by electronic or printed technologies might be formally institutionalised in such policies as open admissions, freedom of selection of what, when and where to learn. Distance education organisations may indeed limit the extent of their openness, but traditionally they have shown a strong bias towards supporting the freedom of individual learners to exercise choice over one or more of the main processes of their learning. Typically this involves helping learners take responsibility for aspects such as what they learn, how they learn, where they learn, how quickly they learn, who to turn to for help and whether, when and where to have their learning assessed.

The openness of distance education is also seen in relatively flexible organisational structures, delivery and communication patterns, and the use of various technologies in support of learning. Open and distance learning is usually contrasted with "conventional" or "face-to-face" education, which may be described as the form of education which takes place in a classroom or an auditorium. However, both "distance" and "face-to-face" education are labels covering a wide range of variations and methods.

Face-to-face education may vary along a continuum from one-to-one tutorials, group activities, seminars and classroom teaching to lectures for large audiences. In each case different educational philosophies may be applied and different methods may be used. Face-to-face education may be supported by a range of media, and may be combined with periods of independent study. In a similar way, distance education has a variety of forms, according to the underlying educational philosophy, organisational approach and choice of technology, and distance educators may incorporate into their programmes an element of face-to-face teaching. The historical evolution of distance education has been in four main phases, each with its own organisational form derived from the main form of communication.

Correspondence systems originated at the end of the nineteenth century, and are still the most widely used form of distance education in less developed countries. Based around a study material in printed text and often accompanied by audio and video components such as records and slides, interaction in the correspondence method is by letters and other written or printed material sent through postal systems.

Educational television and radio systems use various delivery technologies—terrestrial, satellite, and cable television and radio—to deliver live or recorded lectures to both individual home-based learners and groups of learners in remote classrooms where some face-to-face support might be provided. Some systems offered limited audio or video-conferencing links back to the lecturer or a moderator at a central point.

Multimedia systems encompass text, audio, video, and computer-based materials, and usually some face-to-face learner support delivered to both individuals and groups. In this approach, which is that used by the open universities, instruction is no longer an individual's work, but the work of teams of specialists,—media specialists, information specialists, instructional design specialists, and learning specialists. Programmes are prepared for distribution over large numbers of learners, usually located across a whole country.

Internet-based systems in which multimedia (text, audio, video and computer-based) materials in electronic format are delivered to individuals through computers, along with access to databases and electronic libraries, and which enable teacher-student and student-student, one-to-one, one-to-many, and many-to-many interactions, synchronously or asynchronously, through e-mail, computer conferences, bulletin boards, etc. Just as each previous generation of technology, i.e. correspondence, broadcast and narrowcast audio and video, and multimedia systems, produced its particular form of distance learning organisation, so the spread of broadband Internet communication is stimulating new types of educational organisations and also stimulating rethinking about the effectiveness of the older ones. Thus the new technologies are being taken up with equal enthusiasm by open universities, correspondence schools, established "dual mode" institutions and by those now converting to dual mode status, as well as by newly emerging "single mode", purely electronic universities.

"Single mode" institutions are those in which distance education is the sole mission, to which teachers and administrative staff are exclusively dedicated. Course development, instruction, evaluation and other educational processes are tailored to the distant learner.

In *"dual mode" institutions* there may be an administrative staff whose sole responsibilities are distance education, but usually it is the teachers of the parent body who provide the teaching. There is some allowance for distance teaching methods in course design, instruction and evaluation and teachers may have some special training. The most common distance learning design process is the "author-editor" model; each course is based on a study material prepared by a single course writer. Where the Internet is available the study material may be accessed online rather than in hard copy.

Distance learning consortia consist of two or more distance learning institutions who share in either the design or delivery of programmes, or both. Increasingly in many countries teachers in conventional institutions are required to teach at a distance as a responsibility added to their normal duties. Teachers have little training in distance methods. Such programmes may not have their own administrative or learner support services and there are relatively low levels of tailoring of course design, instruction and evaluation to the distant learner.

Non-traditional providers, including private profit-oriented new companies are entering the global market, selling educational services online, especially to adult learners in the labour force. For-profit universities are able to raise money in stock offerings tied to their distance education programmes.

Some for-profit online programmes are growing twice as fast as the dual mode institution's face-to-face programmes, attracting students from more than a score of different countries. Some traditional education institutions are responding to such competition by establishing their own for-profit affiliates, while corporations have established their own in-house systems to meet their own needs for "just-in-time" and "just-enough' education.

1.1 COMPONENTS OF DISTANCE LEARNING SYSTEMS

It is the *mission* of a distance learning system that defines its role within the context of national policy. The mission may be directed towards particular purposes, target groups, regions, sectors or levels of education and training, and driven by particular values and philosophies of learning and education. The mission statement of a public institution will be part of a national policy, while the mission of private organisations may fulfil subsidiary functions in relation to the public institutions. On the other hand, private organisations must respond to the needs of particular market segments, especially of the labour market, both quickly and efficiently.

Courses and curricula define the profile of a system or institution. They should be related to the mission and to defined needs or markets. Many distance education systems provide courses in preparation for examinations and degrees which are equivalent or similar to those offered by conventional institutions, and subject to similar regulations as regards content, admission and assessment.

Teaching strategies and techniques depend partly on the type of programme and the needs they are designed to meet, but they also depend on the educational philosophy and values of the particular system, and the educational characteristics and potential of the technologies used. There may be a connection between teaching strategies, economy and the choice of technology.

Learning materials and resources are essential components in all distance learning systems. Comprehensive, well designed materials may stimulate self-directed learning and thus influence the quality of the system as a whole. Design, development and production of materials are often considered as a sub-system in distance teaching organisations. Previously produced, existing materials, textbooks, software etc. may be used but in most cases each programme benefits from having specifically designed learning materials.

Communication between teachers and learners is a necessary component in distance education, as in all other forms of education. Communication technologies distribute messages in text, still and moving images, and sound. Knowledge-generating messages may be communicated to large numbers of learners, either synchronously or asynchronously, "pushed" by broadcasting or accessed on demand through audio/video players or Internet. As these devices change, so the quality and nature of the messages will change. Thus, new Internet devices will make it possible on the one hand for larger numbers of people to share a common learning experience, in real time, or on the other, to enable an individual learner to have a unique personal interaction with a teacher or with another learner, no matter where located. More importantly these experiences, since they do not depend on physical access, can be of much higher quality than were possible before. They will increasingly be available on a common platform, as bandwidth limitations become less significant than at present.

Communication serves two purposes. One is the distribution of information. This delivery system may comprise both distribution of pre-packaged material and transmission of synchronous or broadcast programmes, lectures etc. The second role of communication is the crucial component of all education which is the *interaction between teachers and learners*, and, where possible, *between learners* also. In some forms of distance education this learner-learner interaction is practically nonexistent, but in most cases it is considered important and may be provided in different ways. Often students meet together physically in groups, some times connected with other forms of local support. New technologies allow the organisation of "virtual groups", and in countries where access to the Internet is common, this is the fastest growing approach to distance teaching.

Support delivered locally is a common component in most single mode institutions. A letter, a telephone call or an e-mail message is of course delivered locally and is more likely to be the means of learner support in dual mode institutions. What is meant here is, however, support in a form that allows some kind of direct (face-to-face) interaction between the learner and a teacher or a mentor/facilitator. This component may be organised completely as face-to-face events, or in combination with communication at a distance (teleconferences etc.). Local support is usually given in a study centre or resource centre. The centre may also offer access to other learning resources, equipment etc.

The *student and staff management* sub-system is often distinguished from the course materials sub-system. From an administrative perspective the student and staff management sub-system comprises admission, allocation to courses and student services, administering the learning and teaching procedures, assignments and assessment, monitoring drop-out and completion, and examinations. Staff may be contracted on a part-time basis or may be in the core faculty in the case of a dual mode institution, but in either case they have to be recruited, trained and monitored. A range of other experts with different qualifications is also needed, either as full-time staff or as external consultants: planners, instructional designers, developers and producers, researchers, media experts, marketing experts and administrative staff.

Effective *management and administration* needs not only competent staff, but also well designed, efficient administrative systems and routines, planning and monitoring systems, budgetary and accounting systems etc. Many of these will be quite different from the corresponding systems needed in the management of other forms of education.

The requirements of *housing and equipment* may also be very different from conventional education institutions. A single mode distance learning system has no residential students, and thus there is little need for classrooms, lecture theatres etc. at the central location. Such facilities may be needed locally, and are often provided in co-operation with local institutions. At the central location there will be need for production facilities and storage capacity, although some decentralised production is also possible. In a dual mode institution these distance education facilities have to be accommodated alongside the space dedicated to the institution's primary mission.

Finally, *evaluation* should be a component, in order to provide information relevant to the adjustment of the roles and operation of system components, and in order to secure their optimal contribution and development. The success of any distance education institution, dual or single mode, is highly dependent on the efficiency and effectiveness of the monitoring and evaluation system, without which it may be impossible for administrators to be aware of problems in the system until the system itself breaks down. It is not possible to rely upon the kind of informal, unstructured feedback that may be sufficient in the conventional classroom.

1.2. ROLE OF TECHNOLOGY IN DISTANCE LEARNING

The use of technology to aid in the processing and communication of information is not new; it is at least as old as writing. However, over the last 50 years, the development of a range of technologies has accelerated exponentially, mainly due to the invention of digital electronics. A vital recent development has been the convergence of technology concerned mainly with the processing of information with that which deals mainly with its communication. This is clearly seen in the emergence of the Internet, whereby the processing power in each office and school can easily be connected, and can communicate with corresponding systems anywhere else in the world. The greater extent to which this integration is realised, the more blurred such distinctions become. We can reach the point where the user does not know whether the information resource being accessed is held on the local machine—and more significantly does not care where it comes from.

The importance of the use of the resources and technologies of the Internet in education is obvious today. It has been shown that the use of the Internet in the sphere of organisation and management of education leads to the increase of education accessibility on a global scale, and may lead to the growth of economic efficiency of an educational institution's activity. All developed countries of the world have more or less extensive programmes of Internet development in the sphere of education. The overwhelming majority of developing countries, despite difficulties, problems and fears, seek as far as possible to take part in the formation of the global educational community. In doing so, the systematisation and analysis of the experience of Internet usage in education becomes an urgent issue for each country and the global community as a whole.

Taking the huge scale of the Internet into account, the creation of mechanisms designed for effective navigation of the Internet, and the collection, analysis, exchange and distribution of information for the specific use of education acquires great importance. However, despite the outstanding progress made in some countries in the creation of universal information retrieval systems and specialised information systems for education, neither set of systems taken separately can provide a complete service. It has usually been found that only 2 or 3 out of 20 current Internet-applications are used in most educational institutions. Further, this situation arises from a lack of information rather than a lack of finance.

A powerful tool for the solution of the resultant problems can however be provided on the basis of the cooperation between such systems. The specialised information system "Education via the Internet" within the framework of UNESCO programme activity may become one of a group of permanent international tools of cooperation. The application of the Internet in education is understood as the use of various Internet-technologies for the solution of various educational tasks, namely, teaching, learning and management of the educational process. The systematic analysis of experiences as they have hitherto been identified and defined in using the Internet in education provides an opportunity for comparison and generalisation.

1.2.1 Web-based Learning

The Web potentially offers a worldwide forum in which to teach courses. One can assume, for example, that each student at any time has an excellent encyclopaedia at his or her disposal. Course material can be dynamically updated. Course text, examples and exercises can be interactive in the sense of immediately illustrating equations with graphs, changing parameters and seeing the results, linking to other web-sites according to the interests of the student.

The Web-based learning model is essentially free from limitations of space and time while it reaches students around the world with great ease. In addition, the Web-based learning model offers students a wealth of information that was never possible in the classical model. For example, the student who suddenly becomes interested in what kind of music was composed during Newton's lifetime could link to that information, even though the instructor may not know how to answer such a query. The possibility of linking to information worldwide in a multitude of formats creates a remarkably rich medium for learning.

Web-based courseware is not merely an electronic duplicate of the original course material. It represents a new type of educational materials which takes full advantage of the emerging Web and multimedia technologies in order to achieve an effective yet enjoyable learning process. Thus, complex concepts are introduced in innovative ways. Full linking to vast resources available worldwide introduces new levels of value to the courseware.

A Web-based course is envisioned as a dynamically-evolving resource that will prove beneficial to both students and teachers alike. In the light of these foregoing remarks, it is evident that the design of a Web-based course is a multifaceted process that closely resembles that of movie making in cinema productions. That is, a Web-based course is developed through the efforts of a team of professionals with a complementary range of skills, as opposed to classical course design, which is typically developed by faculty alone.

The richness of modern Web and multimedia technologies allow for unlimited creativity when it comes to electronic courseware development. Such richness offers educators new opportunities to develop very interesting course material while it also poses a substantial challenge in that it requires faculty to rethink their own course offerings in the light of the new technologies.

One of the first areas that requires change is higher education's perception of technology as it relates to its mission. For the past decade, most attempts to use technology in higher education have been very haphazard: systems have been designed only to automate existing processes, computers have been thought of as strictly computational devices, and desktop workstations have not accomplished much more than replacing the typewriter and the adding machine.

Now-a-days however, technology is creating a new educational platform and is reconfiguring the way a student learns. Networked learning—accessing libraries, scholars, networks, and information worldwide—is evolving. In the light of this, one important question needs to be considered—what is the mission of higher education? It can be said that education is a discovery process, and its mission is to provide the widest repertoire of possibilities for a student entering a learning situation.

Technology can realise this ambition, and because of it a student's educational experience can be immeasurably richer. Various typologies of Internet Applications in Education (IAE) have been proposed in the literature in recent years. Two main approaches to the segmentation of this project-domain have been revealed through the analysis of recent experience. The technology-oriented approach is the most widespread. For example, statistical research on the use of the electronic communication in open and distance learning, conducted by UNESCO in 1995, has identified the following types of applied telecommunication media in educational programmes: telephone; fax; audio-conference; video-conference; electronic mail; access to databases.

1.2.2. Individualised Learning

We should not underestimate the prevalence and importance of "person-to-person" type of communications on the Net. For a long time electronic mail has remained the only Internet application in education. Data submitted in the above-mentioned UNESCO survey reveals that electronic mail is still the most frequently used computer technology in open and distance learning.

A relatively new phenomenon in educational communications is the newly established practice of learners speaking directly to experts in one or another field (which can already be considered as a consequence of the increase in the level of communication skills among learners actively using the Internet). On the Net, there are a number of centres such as Yahoo! Yahooligans! School Bell; Homework Answers; and Ask a Scientist. By addressing enquiries to these centres learners can receive, via e-mail, answers to their questions on a particular theme.

1.2.3. Group Learning and Teaching via Internet

An online lecture or presentation of teaching material published on the Net becomes accessible to many learners. At the first stage of IAE implementation, the most common technology for this "communications paradigm" was the electronic bulletin board (BBS) and electronic mail discussion lists (listservs), where course notes were given with "read-only" access for students. Since the extensive implementation of interactive WWW technologies in the distribution of educational information, various forms of courses on the WWW have become common. WWW technologies have made it possible for materials on the Net to be published with ease. Other learners can thus become the source of information for the learner.

1.2.4. Collaborative Activities

The advantages provided by the Internet in the organisation of cooperation are suggested by its very nature. As is well known, the WWW was created as an environment specifically designed for collaborative work on documents by groups of researchers remote from each other. The further development of Internet technologies has provided the opportunity for joint use and the editing of textual materials, and also of audio- and video-sequences. Problems of legislative and public control over Internet contents are a part of a general problem, which can be identified as the trans-cultural nature of the Net. It can offer a considerable challenge for the cultural identity of the nations of the world. As was mentioned at the Second UNESCO-ACEID Conference, organised by UNESCO-ACEID in cooperation with the Ministry of Education of Thailand in Bangkok, 1996, new technologies pose in particular questions of their influence on the culture. In some countries, governments have a negative view of Internet access since it can break the culture. The limited capacity of data delivery channels creates technical restrictions for enquiries to data and knowledge bases, especially those of a multimedia nature.

1.2.5. Institutional Impact of Internet-technologies

The application of Internet-technologies to educational systems at different levels has a significant impact on the development of open and distance learning-related forms of teaching. Traditional methods of delivery of educational materials and organisation of feedback to learners—such as mail and telephone—are increasingly being replaced by electronic mail and the WWW. Educational institutions of different types and educational levels now provide greater or lesser elements of their teaching through the WWW.

An example of the use of Internet-technologies in higher education is represented by those specialised distance education institutions delivering a considerable part of educational materials through the WWW. Further, many traditional higher education establishments have introduced separate distance courses.

Although open and distance learning at the current time is predominantly represented in higher education, it is gradually also beginning to be used in high schools. Owston singles out three areas of secondary education where this has taken place. Firstly, in home education: as a result of the availability of WWW resources, children suffer to a lesser extent from shortage of educational materials and a lack of dialogue with classmates—two main disadvantages of home education. Secondly, alternative education arising in the context of freedom of choice of school is sometimes remote from the place of residence of a pupil. Thirdly, it is possible to offer extra courses to pupils in conventional schools, in particular in preparation for entry to higher education institutions.

1.3. CONTRIBUTIONS OF DISTANCE LEARNING

Open and distance learning is used for a wide range of purposes. This section will summarise some of the main areas and sectors where open and distance learning has made major contributions.

1.3.1. General Education

Distance education can be used at primary and secondary education levels to provide both in-school and out-of-school programmes. In-school distance education programmes are used to support teaching in schools when learning materials are lacking, or where enrichment is thought to be desirable. They may also be used where teachers do not have formal qualifications, or to support subjects where the number of pupils is too small to be able to organise conventional teaching. A variety of approaches are used, including Interactive Radio Instruction (IRI), schools radio, educational television through terrestrial and satellite networks, multimedia schemes delivered through satellite, and Web-based delivery of multimedia schemes. The materials may be designed for young children or for adolescents and adults.

Distance education is used in out-of school programmes both at primary and secondary level to educate school-age children and youth who are unable to attend ordinary schools, including those who are disabled, suffering from long-term illness, or living in remote areas or living outside their own countries. These programmes generally use correspondence methods. Some programmes are designed to provide lessons that parents can use to teach their own children. Other programmes are designed to be supported by teachers, with parents providing direct supervision. Such programmes may, for example, combine correspondence education with two-way radio contact. As well as focusing on isolated individuals, out-of-school programmes can also be directed at nomadic and itinerant groups. They may also be directed at youths and adults who dropped out of initial formal education, and for whom distance education represents a convenient opportunity at a later stage of their life. Open schools, which use a variety of approaches (print, broadcast, face-to-face and other media), are of particular interest to high population countries. Those aimed at children offer the same curriculum as normal state schools: equivalency of standards and of qualifications offered is important to their legitimacy.

Out of school programmes for adults tend to provide basic education through a range of models. Both radio schools and open schools targeting adults tend to provide a complementary—often vocational or socially-directed—curriculum, as opposed to the state-controlled curricula of the primary school.

1.3.2. Teacher Education

Teacher education is an important area where distance education has been used extensively to provide pre-service teacher preparation, upgrading of academic qualifications, and in-service continuing professional development in particular subjects, content areas and instructional methods. Many examples, particularly from both developing and developed countries, show that teacher training at a distance may reach large groups of teachers and may have profound impact on the development of national education systems. Examples include distance learning initiatives in countries such as

Burkina Faso, Chile, China, India, Mongolia, Nigeria, and South Africa to prepare new teachers or upgrade skills of the existing teaching force. The use of open and distance learning for teacher education is therefore a crucial strategy when expansion or quality improvement is needed in the public education system.

Distance education may play an increasingly important role during this decade in helping address the growing shortage of teachers, educational administrators and other educational professionals experienced in both developing and developed countries. Developed countries are using the Internet as the principal or supplementary means of providing both pre-service and in-service teacher education. There is a growing number of high quality Web-based professional development resources available for educators globally.

The current and emerging communication and information technologies provide unique opportunities to continue the professional development of teachers and other educators. The Web provides teachers with incredibly rich instructional and information resources to enhance their instruction and professional skills and the possibility of on-demand, just-in-time professional development without leaving their classrooms.

The Web also provides opportunities for online mentoring and support of novice teachers during their first year of teaching and to develop online communities of practice. Virtual Web-based environments for teachers now enable them to seek help from other teachers, locally, nationally, or globally in solving classroom problems, sharing lesson plans and materials, interacting with experts in particular fields, and in planning collaborative curriculum development projects. The latter may be particularly important in nations in which educational expertise in specific knowledge domains or instructional practices is scarce and distributed.

Distance education may also play a major role in upgrading the knowledge and skills of teacher educators both in higher education and educational agencies. Web-based resources and tutorials may assist teaching faculty and teacher educators in upgrading their knowledge and skills in areas such as the new technology tools for learning in order that they may infuse and model the use of technology in the courses they offer to future teachers. A particular advantage of distance education is that it is makes teacher preparation and professional development programmes accessible to indigenous peoples and others located in remote, rural areas who do not have convenient access to higher education institutions and where there is often a shortage of well-prepared teachers and other educational professionals.

Often, when individuals must leave their communities to attend higher education institutions in urban areas, they do not return upon completion of their education. In contrast, distance education may help develop qualified teachers and other educational professionals among members of the local community who are also best able to adapt or develop curriculum resources that meet national standards but also reflect and integrate local culture and indigenous knowledge. Such educators are best able to make the learning process more relevant to their students. By developing local educators, distance education may also play a significant role in contributing to the economic development of the community.

It is recognised that in many developing countries access to the Web in local schools is not possible. However, the Web may provide an important resource for teacher education institutions and agencies and centres that provide professional development to teachers in the country. In countries with limited access to technology infrastructure, radio, television and print-based materials are used to address teacher education needs. The China Television Teacher's College, a part of the China Central Radio and Television University, uses television-based distance education to prepare new teachers and provide a range of distance education professional development programmes to primary and secondary teachers, principals and administrators.

Brazil's national distance education system, PROFORMAÇÃO, is used to provide initial training to unqualified preschool and primary education teachers and combines self-study and biweekly workshops using print-based and video materials. Other countries with limited technology facilities also rely heavily on print-based materials as well as radio and other media options. India, for example, uses print-based materials, audio and video cassettes, coupled with optional face-to-face tutorials in local study centres, to provide a comprehensive child development certification programme for teachers.

Mongolia uses radio and print-based materials as part of the strategy to help primary teachers transform the teaching-learning process. South Africa is using interactive radio to support teachers of English as a second language. The above examples illustrate some of the ways the technology resources available within each country may be used to provide pre-service and in-service teacher education.

Finally, distance education and the new tools for learning may serve as a catalyst for changing teaching practices, the roles of teachers and students as part of an overall strategy for systemic change of the educational system to reflect current knowledge on human learning and to help the educational system be more responsive to local and national needs as well as global trends.

1.3.3. Vocational and Continuing Education

Technical and vocational education have in recent years played important roles, not only in contributing to the improvement of productivity of a national labour market, but also in assisting individuals to improve their employment prospects in rapidly changing socioeconomic conditions. In this regard, the role of open and distance learning in the field of technical and vocational education is significant. It has two main functions: to respond effectively to the growing demand of working adults or any others who have difficulties in getting training in conventional education because of lack of flexibility in the timing and location of courses; to provide an opportunity for the empowerment of those most disadvantaged by existing provision—the unemployed, the disabled, women and ethnic minorities.

Open and distance learning in the field of technical and vocational education makes up a mixed and complex picture. It may include experimental work and hands-on training as an integral element. It has often been developed by private institutions and enterprises, and makes an important contribution to human development. It is often necessary to supplement distance learning with intensive experimental work and hands-on training through residential schools, home experiment kits, etc. Examples could also be mentioned from within the public sector. Electronically supported open and distance learning programmes using the World Wide Web are now substantially employed in technical, vocational and professional education. Many countries have developed vocational, polytechnic and other types of short-cycle colleges, sometimes spanning both secondary and post-secondary levels.

In addition to management, business studies and technician training, one may also mention training for agriculture and for public administration and health services as important areas. Continuing education and training is an expanding field in which open and distance learning is used to a great extent. The need for recurrent and continuous updating of knowledge and skills is recognised as a fundamental demand in society today, and open and distance learning with its decentralised and flexible delivery and its modular structure of courses and curricula has become an obvious way of meeting this need.

Open and distance learning institutions offer their courses and programmes for this purpose, and they are developing particular courses for particular needs. Cooperation and partnerships between enterprises, professional bodies and distance teaching institutions are growing, and consortia and special training institutions have been established in order to serve particular trades and professions with continuing education courses.

1.3.4. Non-formal Education

Although distance education has been used to considerable effect in the non-formal and community development sectors of education, it is probably true to say that its potential has never been fully realised. Enthusiasm for basic adult education grew in the 1960s and 1970s just as technology began to be used more widely in education in developed countries. Mass communication methods, often linked with some kind of group meetings and face-to-face support, were seen as one way of delivering a wide range of educational and skills programmes in support of agriculture, health and nutrition, political education (in the emergent democracies of the post-colonial period), and development- and employment-related projects, to large numbers of adults.

An early and influential prototype—the Canadian Farm Forums of the 1940s—suggested a way forward through the motto "Read, listen, discuss, act". This approach was later used in India and Ghana. Radio campaigns were another early and influential model. The idea was to deliver short, highly intensive campaigns to support major development ends.

Research suggested, however, that audiences were often unresponsive, projects often inappropriate, and the lack of resources to follow up the campaigns meant that information can not be turned into action—with the result that campaigns of this kind were not repeated. However, there is much anecdotal evidence of the effectiveness of small-scale non-formal education projects using radio—for example, to support health care in Sudan and rural women in Mongolia. Latterly radio and television dramas have been used in countries such as Gambia and Nigeria as a means of educating people about health issues such as family planning and HIV/AIDS. Indeed, radio in particular has a powerful role to play in non-formal education.

Some of the early projects were designed to break free of those parts of the school syllabus that are irrelevant to adults, and instead offer a curriculum of more practical use to their audiences, but this thrust was not developed as much as it might have been in the face of economic findings that suggested that the case for investment in non-formal education was not as strong as that for investing in projects delivering the formal curriculum.

As a result the rapid development of non-formal education projects was curbed as enthusiasm for the idea that mass communication systems should be mobilised for development, and the financial resources that followed, began to wane. Nevertheless, the anecdotal evidence suggests that there are many successful but largely unreported and often formally unevaluated projects run by the extension services of ministries of health, agriculture, and labour, and by NGOs.

One relatively well reported project is the African Institute for Economic and Social Development (INADES), which is headquartered in the Côte d'Ivoire, and operates as semi-autonomous efforts across eight francophone and two anglophone countries. It has done much to provide education aimed at farmers, agricultural extension agents, and women, using various approaches, including distance education (largely correspondence lessons and assignments). Participants are predominantly male though special efforts are made to reach out to women farmers, and indeed most of the non-literate participants are women.

Projects are delivered through a vast range of organisational structures involving public community development services, popular movements and organisations, churches and religious organisations, charitable foundations and organisations, private institutions and government-funded schools, colleges and universities—but all in essence develop centrally produced materials that can then be used in distributed sites to deliver non-formal education locally to adults. The most common approaches involve print sometimes combined with correspondence teaching, some form of broadcasts or recorded media—often radio/audio, coupled with some form of face-to-face support—even extending as in the Gobi Desert Women's Project to home visits by tutors to learners. The learners often come from the more marginalised sectors of society, and as a result have low levels of previous formal education or none at all.

In this connection it is worth noting that programmes aimed at illiterates and new literates have to be designed carefully to ensure that such learners can benefit from the programme. This requires a cadre of support workers. Generally learners enrol to achieve a particular learning objective, and wish to progress quickly. These characteristics determine the curricula, which are usually focused on specific issues to do with social and community education, health and family, and economic and earnings-related education, including agriculture. Moreover, projects can support equity goals—though this can be undermined by policies that require learners to pay for materials and services. The evidence suggests that projccts can be delivered cost-efficienlly, and that they can be effective, particularly where—bottom up community dialogue—leads to the successful integration of such programmes into the wider development needs of a society.

1.3.5. Higher Education

There are more distance learning courses offered at the tertiary level than at any other. This has been the case since the invention of the distance education method near the end of the nineteenth century when the use of new technology (i.e. national rail systems that supported national postal systems) made it possible to deliver higher education beyond the boundaries of the campus, especially in such "new" and large nations as the United States, Canada, Australia, South Africa, and Russia. In turn these countries led the way in the use of radio for university level teaching, then television, and today the Internet. In these nations the preferred organisational form was, and remains, the dual mode university.

The Internet has attracted the attention of university academics to the idea of distance teaching in a way that no previous technology managed to do. Together with the pressure from new competitors for student enrolment, this enthusiasm for technology explains the growing number of traditional universities that are converting to dual mode status. Such universities usually teach the same curricula for distance students as for their residential students and subject the students (but not always) to the same entrance requirements and examinations.

The success and expansion of single mode open universities on the one hand, and the transformation of traditional universities to dual mode universities on the other, are important contributions to the diversification and development of higher education systems.

1.4. INNOVATIONS IN DISTANCE LEARNING

Open and distance learning has a major impact on thinking and practice throughout the whole educational system, regarding such critical matters as how students learn, how they can best be taught, and how educational resources might more efficiently be organised to deliver the instruction that is needed.

Open and distance learning is closely linked to innovation in information and communication technologies, to the identification of new learning needs and new ideas about how information may be accessed and applied in the information society. In particular open and distance learning has the potential to enhance a more student-centred and consumer-oriented approach to education, leading in turn to more extensive contact between educational institutions on the one hand and community-based organisations, business and industry on the other.

Innovation in how resources are organised is essential, and open and distance learning has demonstrated how the labour (i.e. teacher) to capital (i.e. technology) ratio can be improved to lead to greater efficiency. Unlike open and distance learning, conventional schools and universities are still organised on the assumption that learning is dependent on a single informed person imparting information by word of mouth to a small group of listeners in a classroom.

A multitude of solitary individuals are responsible for the organisation and control of information, are designers of their courses, manage the instructional process, are testers, motivators, counsellors and evaluators for a handful of learners. Teaching, in other words, remains organised as a craft not a system. With open and distance learning there is greater specialisation of labour and investment in capital to replace certain human activities. It is this different form of structure that makes the technology effective and leads to lowering costs while increasing access.

To bring about this increased efficiency, new national policies and reforms in regulatory frameworks may be needed. Many countries have already engaged in reform of their telecommunications policies, particularly regarding Internet backbone development, and relaxation of the monopolies of publicly owned telecommunications companies. New international partnerships are emerging, not only of telecommunications providers, but also of universities and training institutions, equipment providers, content producers and publishers, software developers, assessment services, credit banks, and library services.

However, the organisational frameworks in which technology is used in education have not been treated to the same radical policy reviews as has the telecommunications infrastructure itself. Other work has to be done to establish policies concerning international trade in educational services and such related matters as institutional accreditation and assessment, certification of learning, intellectual property rights, and incentive structures (tax breaks, subsidies, promotion of public/

private sector collaboration, etc.). While information technology has potential to deliver high quality content more cost-effectively it cannot, nor should it be expected to replace the appropriate use and availability of human helpers in the learning process. As teachers become less information communicators and more knowledge processers, experts in learning rather than content, so technology can help them do their jobs more efficiently provided they are organised into better integrated systems.

Because the economies of large-scale production enable distance education systems to invest larger sums in the design and development of study materials than smaller, conventional teaching institutions, the quality of such materials is usually higher, and this in turn makes for a raising of standards throughout the educational system. This may have a particularly important influence when teachers and professors of conventional institutions become involved in the development or use of these materials, for instance on contract with a distance teaching institution.

The introduction of a distance programme at a conventional university may also lead to curriculum reform and new learning materials for resident students in the same subjects. In some projects distance learning is used systematically to support conventional systems at basic and secondary levels. The potential of distance learning to increase innovation and creativity in conventional education depends on the degree of interaction between distance learning systems and conventional systems. Ideally, there ought to be formal links between such institutions and the conventional system, in order that they may serve as national resource centres. Organisational innovation does not mean setting up new institutions. A new organisational model is that of a network of institutions and individuals that together provide the kind of services delivered by single mode institutions, but on a more flexible and open basis through a process of commissioning.

A small management team is one of two essential requirements for a network; and the other is a significant funding resource that allows the management team to obtain the quality resources needed from wherever they are located. What this approach promises is a very flexible, versatile, responsive system that produces high quality without commitment to ongoing institutional costs, and delivers efficiently by employing the comparative advantage of each institution in a country or region.

A second innovative model is the Independent Study model, which gives learners control of their own learning programmes through use of new technology. This calls for a different type of organisation than was useful when information was stored centrally in a location to which students could travel, or in a distance teaching centre from which they it could be "distributed". Such an organisation could make instructors anywhere available to students anywhere, and could make courses prepared by any institution available to students anywhere.

A student's teachers need no longer be limited to those who assemble in any one place, any more than a Teacher's students would have to assemble in one place. Students could learn wherever they are located from instructional resources wherever they are located. No student would need to take instruction from exactly the same teacher as any other; students could have access to teachers from any state or country at any time and in any combination; they could have access to information resources from any state or country at any time and in any combination. Students also could have universal access to advice and guidance.

1.5. DISTANCE EDUCATION IN INDIA

India developed Open and Distance Education (ODE) system, both at school and higher education levels, in the country to supplement its face-to-face, conventional education system with the objective to provide opportunity for education to larger segment of population.

In order to take care of flexible and learner-centric schooling needs of the masses in the year 1979, a project was started by Country's Central Board of Secondary Education (CBSE), which has now taken the shape of National Institute of Open Schooling (NIOS). It has approximately 1.5 million learners on its roll, which made it the largest Open Schooling organisation of the world. NIOS has international presence and provides access to sustainable and learner-centric quality school education (from basic to senior secondary level), skill up-gradation, training through open and distance learning and ensures convergence of open schooling organisations.

By the 1980s there were 34 universities offering correspondence education through departments designed for that purpose. The first single mode Open University was established in Andhra Pradesh in 1982, followed by the Indira Gandhi National Open University (IGNOU), in 1985, and subsequently in Bihar, Rajasthan, and Maharashtra, Madhya Pradesh, Gujarat, Karnataka, West Bengal, and Uttar Pradesh (established throughout the 1980s and 1990s). The establishment of these single mode distance education universities was stimulated by the government's intention to democratise education and make it lifelong. The initiative did not discourage the expansion at the same time of correspondence programmes in dual mode universities. The year 1995 witnessed the enrolment of 200,000 students in open and distance learning, accounting for 3% of total higher education enrolment.

The Indira Gandhi National Open University (IGNOU), the biggest open learning university in Asia provides innovative and need based general as well as continuing education to: the person from disadvantaged groups, physically challenged; homemakers; and, those, who are based in remote areas for their educational and professional development.

The university practises a flexible and open system of education in regard to methods and place of learning, combination of courses and eligibility for enrolment, age for entry and methods of evaluation, etc. IGNOU has adopted an integrated strategy for imparting instruction. This consists of providing print materials, audio-video tapes, broadcast on radio and educational TV Channels, teleconferencing, video conference as also the face-to-face counselling, at its study centres located throughout the country. The University has adopted the method of continuous assessment and term-end examination for evaluation of the performance of its students enrolled in various subjects.

IGNOU has a large number of programmes, ranging from purely academic to technical, professional and vocational at various levels leading to award of: Competency Certificates; Diplomas; and Bachelor's, Master's and Doctor's degree to successful candidates. Many of these programmes are modular in nature. In the year 2007, the University has offered 129 programmes, which included 16 Doctoral level, 18 Master's level, 13 Bachelor's level, 21 Post-Graduate Diploma level, 22 Diploma level and 39 Certificate and Awareness level programmes. The University has fresh enrolment of about half million students during the academic year 2008-09. The student support system of IGNOU now consists of a network of 59 Regional Centres, 5 Sub-

Regional Centres, 1468 Study Centres and 37 Overseas Centres. The University has 354 teaching and 1138 non-teaching staff to its strength. To implement all its programmes, IGNOU has spent Rs. 236.00 crores during the financial year 2006-07.

ODE System of the country, in the higher education sector, has one national Open University (IGNOU), 13 State Open Universities (SOUs), one Open University in the private sector. In addition to this, there are approximately 140 dual mode universities (offering education through conventional face-to-face as well as distance mode through their Directorates of Distance Education (DDEs). The above said SOUs and DDEs have enrolled approximately one million fresh students in the academic year 2008-09.

IGNOU is fulfilling its mandate of promotion of ODE Systems and coordination of standard in such Systems in country through its authority, the Distance Education Council (DEC). The Council (DEC) has extended technical and financial support to Open and Distance Education Institutes (ODIs) for development of technological infrastructure, institutional reform, professional development and training, student support services, computerised and networking for improvement of quality of education. During the year 2007-08, DEC has provided financial assistance to 13 SOUs and 44 DDEs in order to promote and coordinate the standards in ODE system in the country. DEC also provides research grant on topics of contemporary relevance, travel grants to individuals to attend international conferences and financial support to Open and Distance Education Institutes for organising seminar. Most open and distance learning universities in India follow the model of the UK Open University. They coordinate communication and collaboration through the Distance Education Council (DEC), founded in 1992. DEC is responsible for the promotion, coordination, and the maintenance of quality and standards.

A range of factors including emerging Information and Communication Technologies, liberalisation, privatisation and globalisation have amplified the demand for open and distance learning. While the government is responsible for more than 90% of open and distance learning funding, plans are underway to involve the private sector more closely, especially through permitting the increase of fees.

1.6. DISTANCE EDUCATION: GLOBAL TRENDS

Considering the challenges of education and development, both in developing and developed countries, it is not surprising that open and distance learning is often seen as an important new approach and strategy which could make a significant contribution towards resolving problems of access, quality and equity. When conventional systems and approaches cannot meet the needs, it is necessary to look for new strategies. Confidence seems to be growing that open and distance learning is such a strategy.

Examples of this growing confidence can be found in many countries. For example, it has been recommended that distance education efforts in the nine high-population countries, focus on "expanding work for school equivalence, for teacher education, and for non-formal education, especially in relation to health.. Strategies for all these areas have been developed that could usefully be applied in most if not all of the E-9 countries. Low-tech and broadcasting strategies figure strongly but there are also a growing range of projects which make innovative use of the new information technologies.

The European Union has in recent years consistently increased distance education components of its educational programmes, and has included open and distance learning explicitly in its Maastricht Treaty. In Central and Eastern Europe, distance education is seen as an important means of supporting the transformation process towards democratic and market-oriented societies. Similar initiatives and statements are forthcoming from a wide range of individual countries as well as from regional and international organisations and agencies.This does not mean that distance teaching institutions escape all financial constraints and cutbacks. In developing countries the general lack of resources in the economy often prevents distance education programmes from being sustained, developed and extended. In addition to the general objective of increased productivity, and usually reluctant to take money away from established educational interests, governments want to have an increasing proportion of expenditure for open and distance learning to be paid by the students through fees.

At the same time, in increasingly market-oriented educational systems, conventional institutions are to a greater extent using some form of open and distance learning as a means of extending their markets. Strategic alliances are being formed between educational and private sector institutions of various kinds. This means that the traditional distinctions between various types of providers (distance—conventional, public—private) are being blurred, particularly within vocational and continuing education and training. Technological development allows for new paradigms of access and new delivery systems, linked to new types of demand.

Continuous miniaturisation of equipment, reduced costs, increased user flexibility, portability and integration offer a whole range of new opportunities.

These changes can either lead to more effective centralised systems of development, and the distribution of educational services and software. They can also support a more open "networked society" with greater variation and more equitable access to educational resources through a network infrastructure. The direction of this development will be strongly influenced by the willingness of governments to provide leadership and coordination concerning network development and access (network here referring not only to technological networks, but networks of educational providers whose services are delivered via the technology).

New technology also means that distance learners are not as highly reliant on the quality of pre-produced packages of course materials or programmes as they were. Technology permits more learner-instructor and learner-learner communication and dialogue and thus a high degree of individualisation of learning and learner construction of knowledge. Nevertheless the quality of the learning programme will depend on well designed instructional materials as well as the ability of the instructor to facilitate such knowledge construction. This puts a high premium on teachers being adequately grounded and trained in distance education methods. Finally, the trend towards internationalisation is clear. In addition to the political and economic driving forces, the internationalisation of distance education is enhanced by its links to Information and Communication Technologies (ICTs).

For instance, educational software is often international, and satellites and electronic networks allow transmission and communication across national borders. The "global classroom" is no longer a concept only of our imagination or of the future. There are of course limitations of access for a range of reasons, but international projects and programmes are already quite common.

1.7. DISTANCE EDUCATION AND EDUCATIONAL CHALLENGES

Education has to be considered in its relation to global economic, social and cultural development. There is now little doubt that major changes are occurring in the world economy, mainly due to the expansion of new information-bearing technologies. In what has already become known as a knowledge-based society, economic advantage will accrue to countries in which the population acquires competence in processing information into knowledge and applying it in work and everyday life. The importance of knowledge as an essential component of the economy has influenced the increasing interest of governments in human knowledge resource development.

The tendency has been evident in developing as well as developed countries, although the circumstances, priorities and challenges are different. In developing countries, human knowledge resource development through initial and continuing education is not only seen as crucial for economic growth and competitiveness, but also has far-reaching social impact, for example in influencing the birth rate, increasing the independence of women, and improving standards of health and the rural environment. The resources available for the development of knowledge are far from evenly distributed. In spite of a considerable quantitative growth in recent years, there are still intolerable inequalities both between and within nations. There are about 880 million illiterate adults in the world and some 113 million children between 6 and 11 deprived of any schooling at all. In higher education also, inequality in opportunities is expected to continue, especially in view of projected population growth. Besides the insufficiency of opportunity, the low quality of education and its frequently observed irrelevance are also of major concern. Rapid changes in the work-force, unemployment and uncertainty now demand fast-changing, "just in time", continuing and lifelong education.

Linked to most of these problems is the problem of financing. Lack of resources in developing countries is obvious, and becomes more acute as demographic trends increase the need to expand educational provision. The "knowledge divide" is, however, compounded by serious situations in certain regions, and particularly in Sub-Saharan Africa. In this region, the achievement of education systems is often threatened by a series of other problems. In the next few years the most serious of these is likely to be the effect of the HIV/AIDS pandemic, followed by the effects of military conflicts.

Under such conditions, it is unrealistic to expect traditional educational structures to provide an adequate basis for knowledge development. A developing country has to find new methods that will dramatically improve both its children's schooling and its continuing education system. New methods will need new organisational forms, which in turn require rethinking of education and training policies. Strategies that have been recommended include the diversification of the resource base by privatising some educational functions, the use of donations from private sources, and the recovery of costs from users and participants.

Another strategy is to focus on increasing efficiency within the system. Future policy will probably involve structural reform and the limitation of expenditure in the public sector. It is therefore relevant to look not only at new technologies but also alternative systemic approaches in pursuit of increasing access, improving cost-effectiveness and quality, as well as learning outcomes.

The development of a more knowledge-based and service-oriented economy leads to important changes in the organisation of work and the structure of skills needed. New jobs tend to demand new and higher levels of skills, customer-oriented communication, problem solving and entrepreneurial skills. The emergence of more flexible work organisations is clearly linked to the development of technology. One of the new challenges for education is that high-level skills are needed not only by an elite, but by the population in general.

Political, economic and technological developments make up a strong movement towards internationalisation. Increasing integration and interdependence of national economies are followed by attempts towards economic integration at regional levels, e.g. in Europe, South East Asia, North and South America, and East and Southern Africa. International and regional co-operation in education and training is often included in such efforts. Internationalisation is enhanced by the development of information and communication technologies. Thus, international and regional markets for education and training are emerging. This leads not only to increased international awareness and orientation in curricula, but also facilitates the exchange and sharing of expertise and human resources.

Major obstacles to internationalisation are found in the barriers to, and limited recognition of, diplomas and qualifications across national borders. There are also cultural aspects connected with internationalisation. Increased communication underlines the needs for mutual information and understanding of cultural and social contexts. Sometimes cultural and ethnic forces oppose internationalisation, leading to an increase in national, ethnic and regional consciousness and in the extreme to polarisation and fragmentation. The challenge to education is to prepare citizens for a truly international community, without neglecting the richness and the value of cultural variation.

As in every other walk of modern life, the answer to the challenge of education for development will include the use of information and communication technologies, provided the necessary organisational and policy changes can be implemented to make the technologies effective. A range of technological devices is now widely available and relatively cheap. They are accepted and often available for domestic use as well as in the workplace. Governments are concerned that educational institutions become connected to the emerging networks, that curricula include the knowledge of and acquaintance with new technologies, and that teachers are prepared and trained to use these new resources.

In efforts to meet the new and changing demands for education and training, open and distance learning may be seen as an approach that is at least complementary and under certain circumstances an appropriate substitute for the face-to-face methods that still dominate most educational systems. While its benefits can be evaluated by technical, social and economic criteria, distance learning methods also have their own pedagogical merit, leading to different ways of conceiving knowledge generation and acquisition.

The barriers that may be overcome by distance learning include not only geographical distance, but also other confining circumstances, such as personal constraints, cultural and social barriers and lack of educational infrastructure. For the student it is often a cheaper alternative to pursuing a course through conventional methods. Since many people cannot afford to leave their work in order to study, it is important that distance education and training may be combined with work.

For employers, open and distance learning offers the possibility of organising learning and professional development in the workplace itself, which is often more flexible and saves costs of travel, subsistence etc. The use of distance learning often puts both the firm and employees in a position of co-investment (of money and time) in the pursuit of common goals, based on shared values and culture.

Other advantages for the employer include the increased availability of the employee during the course of the training programme, and the portability of training programmes and processes. These advantages to learners and employers are also important features from the perspective of governments. Traditionally, governments have introduced distance education provision in order to: increase access to learning and training opportunity; provide increased opportunities for updating, retraining and personal enrichment; improve cost-effectiveness of educational resources; support the quality and variety of existing educational structures; enhance and consolidate capacity.

In the light of the experiences of the past twenty or more years, there is today recognition of other, related, benefits. Some of these are: balancing inequalities between age groups; extending geographical access to education; delivering educational campaigns and other education for large audiences; providing speedy and efficient training for key target groups; expanding the capacity for education in new and multidisciplinary subject areas; offering the combination of education with work and family life; developing multiple competencies through recurrent and continuing education; enhancing the international dimension of educational experience; improving the quality of existing educational services.

2

Development of Open and Distance Learning in India

Open education is a collective term that refers to forms of education in which knowledge, ideas or important aspects of teaching methodology or infrastructure are shared freely over the internet. It was inspired by related concepts like Creative Commons, Open source, Open data and Open Access, and expands them to include lectures and other courseware.

The essence of Open Learning (OL) lies in its being imparted and received in a non-institutional setting; making use of multimedia packages of distance education like print material, audio and video cassettes, radio and TV programmes, etc.; and supplementing this packaged programme by contact programmes. In the case of vocational courses requiring skill development, some training-practice facilities in work place are to be made available for hands-on experience. OL in common with non-formal education, emphasises flexibility and learner-centredness. However, if non-formal education does not make use of distance education methods, it cannot be termed open learning.

Open learning makes use of distance education methods. However, all distance education is not necessarily open in the sense that the courses it offers are open to all types of applicants. Thus, professional programmes of continuing education, being limited to accredited members of a particular profession are not categorised as open education.

Open or distance education programmes have been operational for over 250 years, mainly in Europe and North America, in the form of 'correspondence education' for adults wishing to secure diplomas, degrees or just skills and information of their special interest. Early in the 20th Century, universalisation of primary education in remote geographical areas was carried out by Australia, Canada and New Zealand, through postal tuition. Later, correspondence education began to cover secondary, higher, and some branches of professional education. The use of radio and television for learning-support brought in the term 'distance education'.

But the establishment of the United Kingdom Open University (UKOU) in 1969, gave a new direction to this field. Along with print-materials, it introduced audio and video materials and a system of personal guidance through contact centres for learners and their counsellors. The thrust of the Open University towards equality of educational opportunity for the forgotten millions such as workers and housewives received appreciation. Soon after, many a 'correspondence' course got converted firstly into' distance education' and then into 'Open Education' using the new style of postal tuition supported by personal contact and multimedia packages of learning materials.

Despite a fairly wide expansion of the school system, the number of out-of-school children and youth is still very large and adult illiteracy also is a nagging problem particularly in developing countries. The full-time institutional system of education takes in only those who do not work and who can afford the price it demands. For those who work and contribute to the economy, for those who have little time to spare for full-time education, alternative paths of entry into education must be opened up in the interest of equity as well as socioeconomic development. This is the rationale of the Open Learning System.

A well-designed open learning system which satisfies the dual demand of educational quality and quantity, creates a network of educational opportunities relevant to the needs and circumstances of the learners and their society, can be a major means for accelerating the pace of development in an age dominated by market forces and by technology as the prime input for securing a better standard of living for all.

In India, the chief concern at present is to wipe out adult illiteracy as fast as possible, improve enrolment, retention and achievement at the elementary and secondary stages, and offer vocational courses and further education of various types interlinked with employment possibilities. In such a situation, we need to profit by global experience by culling out from it the factors which suit our needs and combining them imaginatively with our own formulations. Appropriate open education can help build among our people the attitude of self-reliance and self-confidence which are basic to good performance in the work-place as well as in the side spectrum of sociocultural activities which characterise a progressive society. The time has obviously come to take Open Education seriously and organise it systematically for moving speedily towards education and employment for all.

2.1. DEVELOPMENT OF OPEN EDUCATION IN INDIA

Education being the main stimulator of development, does not end with schooling and that it has to be a lifelong process in order to enable the individual to understand the rapidly changing world of work and the growing complexities of human affairs. The Commission, however, noted that in India masses of people are without schooling, even without effective literacy, numeracy and understanding of changing technology. Besides, many of those who have had the opportunity for schooling, partly or fully, have found their conventional courses irrelevant to developmental needs.

A solid foundation for life-long learning provided through literacy, numeracy and 'techniracy' could lead the learners towards capabilities for independent learning and earning. This should be the trend, according to the Commission, in universalisation of elementary education, adult education and further education. From this angle, the Commission indicated that the school would have to reach out to the entire local community and function as a 'Community Learning Centre', a 'people's school'. To fulfil such a role, it would go beyond educating children, disseminate to the community all essential information, and promote vocational education along with social service for integrating the total community into a dynamic unit of development.

A system of continuing education could be designed by making such schools serve as 'contact centres' to cater to the needs of different groups of learners, namely, those who are able to study part-time and those who are necessarily required to study at home at hours convenient to them, through an Open Learning System. Provision of a variety of continuation courses and teaching-learning arrangements was recommended by the Commission through the school system as well as institutions like the Krishi Vigyan Kendras and Community Polytechnics catering to the needs of productive skill-development in the rural areas. Such 'open-door' facilities, outside the regular working hours, are expected to provide flexible, work related learning opportunities. These could as well form constituent parts of the Education Complex give the lead in organising ad-hoc short courses for youth, adult and even school-pupils. It may be necessary to give further consideration to such vocational centres in order to form an integrated Education Complex serving the goal of 'Education and Development.'

The Education Commission, stressing its developmental view, had looked upon the education system as a flexible and dynamic process, responding to the inter-dependant needs of the learners and their society. A substantial expansion of 'part-time' and 'own-time' courses, at all levels of education, covering academic and vocational as well as cultural studies, could be so planned as to bring within their fold a sizeable proportion of students at the secondary and higher education levels. The National Policy on Education has adopted or adapted many such forward-looking recommendations of the Education Commission.

Many of the recommendations of the Education Commission were filled with insight into the development processes and the kind of manpower required to be produced by education for making India a dynamic, forward-looking, economically productive and socially progressive nation. Some of these recommendations were so much ahead of their times that they were not even understood and, consequently, overlooked. The conflict between convention and innovation is an age-old phenomenon.

2.2. OPEN EDUCATION IN UNIVERSITIES

The conventional attraction for degrees and diplomas and the desire of many a secondary certificate holder to acquire further qualifications while in employment or working for employment led to the demand and provision of 'external' degree courses. Correspondence courses followed, as an improvement. The University Grants Commission formulated guidelines for correspondence courses in Indian Universities. A few Universities relaxed formal qualifications for entrants to correspondence courses. By 1989-90, correspondence courses in various disciplines had been instituted by 38 Universities, at the undergraduate, postgraduate and diploma/certificate levels.

The first Open University in the country was established in Andhra Pradesh in 1982, followed by the establishment of the Indira Gandhi National Open University in 1985. More Open Universities got established thereafter, viz. Kota (1987), Nalanda (1987), and YC Maharashtra Open University, Nashik (1989), Nearly five lakh students are at present enrolled in open and correspondence systems. This constitutes 12 per cent of a total enrolment of about 42 lakhs in higher education. Open universities account for about one fourth of the non-institutional enrolment in higher education, the remaining being in traditional correspondence courses.

In the early 1950's, school broadcasts began to supplement the regular curriculum offered by schools and introduced the idea of learning outside the classroom. Television has been used for curriculum enrichment and instructional purposes, right since its introduction in 1959. In 1975-76, Government launched the Satellite Instructional Television Experiment (SITE) exposing 2330 villages in 20 districts of six States (Andhra Pradesh, Karnataka, Bihar, Orissa, Rajasthan and Madhya Pradesh to specially pre-recorded TV programmes directly transmitted via the ATS-6 Satellite. The TV lessons were supported by instructors. Thus, a new dimension was added to the use of electronic media for teaching-learning. The significance of the experiment lies in two factors, viz.

a) Education began to cover even illiterate adults and schooling got dissociated from childhood, and

b) India became the first large country to make use of Direct Receiving Sets (DRS).

In 1984, the Indian National Satellite (INSAT) Programme was launched for the age group 6 to 8 and 9 to 11 on three days per week, in selected primary school-clusters of Andhra Pradesh, Bihar, Gujarat, Maharashtra, Orissa and UP. For production of software, State Institutes of Educational Technology (SIET), have been established in these States. The Central Institute of Educational Technology (CIET) guides their work. This programme, when evaluated showed shortcomings such as custody and maintenance of TV sets, inadequate dovetailing of lessons with classroom teaching, etc. Where the TV sets have functioned well, a positive impact has been evident.

The Open School is about to become a well-organised movement, especially at the secondary level. The Conference of the Boards of Secondary Education had recommended in 1965, introduction of correspondence courses for out-of-school youth and women. The objective was to help improve the performance of privately appearing candidates, in the certificate Examinations. The Board of Secondary Education, Madhya Pradesh, was the first to start correspondence courses for Intermediate students, in 1965. This was followed by the Secondary Boards in Delhi, Rajasthan, Orissa, UP and Tamil Nadu. By 1985, about one lakh students were enrolled at various grade levels, under this programme.

National Open School

The Open School, established under the Central Board of Secondary Education, New Delhi, in 1979 went several steps ahead of correspondence education. It began open secondary courses in 1981-82 and higher secondary courses in 1988. In 1989, the Open School was converted into National Open School. In 1990, it became its own certifying and examining body. It has on its rolls about 1.5 lakh students.

The number of students enrolled at the secondary and higher secondary stages in correspondence/open education is about 1 per cent of the reported enrolment at these stages. The trend shows that among those enrolled in Open School, girls predominate. The need to offer open education facilities at the secondary stage has received increasing recognition. But information about the possibilities of coverage and quality of open secondary education has not yet fully reached those sections of society where it is most needed. Further course offerings are being designed by the National Open School. Boards of Secondary Education that have recently decided to adopt the NOS model as against traditional correspondence courses, have begun preparations to launch their programmes in collaboration with NOS and one another, thus building a participatory network.

In teacher training, the NCERT and its Regional Colleges have been using self-learning packages for quite some time. More recently, as part of the programme of Mass Orientation of School Teachers, TV programmes helped supplement face-to-face instruction for in-service training.

The approach of NPE, 1986, and the Eighth Plan Working Groups to the OLS may be seen from the extracts given in Annexure III: Policy Precursors of OLS. Open Learning receives support both in the National Policy on Education (1986) and the approach to education in the 8th Plan. The need to organise educational activities in a flexible manner has been recognised for meeting the challenge of preparing human resources capable of handling the multi-faceted socioeconomic tasks thrown up by unforeseen worldwide changes in all spheres of life.

2.3. EDUCATIONAL PLANNING

The document on objectives, thrusts and macro-dimensions of the 8th Plan approved by the NDC in its meeting dated 23 24 December, 1991, has identified the following human resource development factors among its priority objectives:

1. Generation of adequate employment opportunities to achieve full-employment level by the turn of the century.
2. Universalisation of elementary education and complete eradication of illiteracy in the age group 15 to 35. In quantitative terms, this requires:
   (*a*) coverage of 6.5 crores of children in the age group 6-14 in the threefold dimension of enrolment, retention and achievement, with special emphasis on girls and the weaker sections, and
   (*b*) coverage of 10.3 crore adults in the age group 15-35.

Literacy, functionality and awareness which are essential for acquisition of lifeskills and cultivation of the skills and habits of self-learning are the major components of adult education. These cover elementary education as well, from the standpoint of the age-group concerned.

The 8th Plan sets the target of progressive opportunities for employment for all, in a ten-year time span. Generation of additional ten million employment opportunities per year on an average, essentially related to productivity, has been visualised, with emphasis on the rural sector.

Agriculture with regionwise and cropwise diversification, wasteland development, forestry, livestock development, rural non-farm occupations, utilisation of non-conventional energy resources, rural infrastructure such as roads and other means of communication, housing, health, education, and other services, urban informal sector, small scale manufacturing and so on have been identified as the sectors and areas constituting the basic elements of an employment-oriented growth strategy.

In addition, it is proposed to raise the productivity and income levels of those who are at present under-employed or employed at very low levels of skills and income. This would entail the upgradation of skills for self-employment as also for wage-employment and improved access to credit and markets. All this effort requires the foundation of purposeful and flexible education, training and retraining. The employment generation target spells out the job that the education sector would have to undertake. The challenge is unprecedented. The education system must innovate in the direction of human development in all its manifestations, from the level of performance in a locally essential job to that called for in the interest of the highest contribution to universal knowledge.

Placing the country's economy on an even keel is undoubtedly the topmost priority at present. Controlling population growth is an extremely important aspect of this priority. As research has shown, it is the twin instruments of education and employment, operating together, that have helped population control. Especially, it is literacy and further education of rural women along with income generation opportunities through acquisition of skills for using new technologies, that have had a natural impact on family size, keeping it small and healthy.

As Dr. Nafis Sadik of the UN Fund for Population Activities has pointed out, "Women's education in itself has a strong contraceptive effect. Population programmes are part of the whole development package. It is not an either or situation social programmes or development." At the grassroots level the orientation of development personnel would be essential for participation in these efforts for educating and empowering rural women.

It is through the Open System that this retraining of development functionaries would have to be undertaken. It would have to change their values, attitudes and help them absorb the correct concept of development as also the `skills essential for inducing and managing change based' on people's initiatives and participation. Therefore', acquisition of skills and knowledge for generating development would have to be the responsibility of various groups as an interactive process and this would be a major area for providing Open Education.

The 8th Plan approach is convergent with and substantiated by the strategic statement issued by the International Commission on Peace and Food in November, 1991, on "Potentials for increasing agricultural productivity in India." The strategy is based on India's competitive advantages to achieve poverty eradication goals by 2000 A.D. through intensive agriculture, agro-industries, and exports. The programmes would comprise utilisation of proven technologies, creation of a large number of new jobs for unskilled and skilled workers, tapping of the huge market potential, both domestic and foreign, and generation of value-added materials. Profits and savings for capital formation would bolster the economy rapidly. It is clear that for such a strategy to succeed, an appropriately educated and trained work-force is indispensable.

The role of the education system in the above context would be to:

(*a*) Provide education and training as well as orientation of various segments of the population so as to achieve wage-employment/self-employment managerial skills/entrepreneurship.

(b) Build up the capabilities of educational functionaries for achieving universalisation of elementary education and adult literacy, in terms of access, retention and educational achievement;

(c) Make provision for the substantial demand for secondary education and, beyond, resulting from UEE;

(d) Provide diversified academic and vocational education of good quality at the secondary level and beyond so as to meet the emerging needs for personal, social, and economic growth; and

(e) Gear various levels and types of educational opportunities for enhancing the overall quality of life in the national contexts.

2.4. OPEN LEARNING SYSTEM: POSSIBILITIES

Acquisition of life-skills, vocational skills directly contributing to productivity, and inculcation of habits of self learning, could be the major thrusts of Open Education. An education system that is easy of access and responsive to the needs and conditions of the learners in different localities and areas, could gradually emerge in a systematic form if Open Education is offered as the third channel of need-based learning. Being demand-based, the open system would also be costeffective, with an inbuilt dynamism which can keep it related to personal as well as socioeconomic demands which are bound to keep changing rapidly with the onrush of science and technology into all facets of our national life.

Without constant monitoring and mid-course corrections, the OLS cart also become as rigid and inequitous as the institutional system, especially if it merely repeats and mirrors the formal education courses and continues to cater to the client groups that are already being served. However, the National Open School has demonstrated that it is possible, with a deliberate effort, to concentrate on certain priorities. In the last five years, the enrolment of girls in the NOS has risen from 20 per cent to 41 per cent. NOS today has students from literally every State of India, even though its courses are offered only through Hindi and English.

2.4.1. Catering to Prioritised Client Groups

The prioritised client groups to be serviced by OLS may be identified as:

- Girls,
- Women,
- SC/ST,
- Rural and Urban Poor,
- Unemployed,
- Young adults, especially in the age range of 15-35,
- Untrained Teachers,
- Inservice teachers, headmasters and supervisors,
- Employed persons anxious to avail of elementary or secondary or vocational education.

In terms of educational attainments and competencies, the priority would have to be for:

(a) Those with education equivalent to primary schooling or above, but below the secondary, viz. classes VI-VIII.

(b) Those who seek vocational education in order to get a job or better prospects.

(c) Those drop-outs who are under-matriculate, wishing to get a secondary and HSE level education.

(*d*) Those who seek instruction In discrete subjects essential for a job or further education.

2.4.2. Educational Programmes

While the need and feasibility of intervention of OLS at secondary and tertiary levels, as regards academic as well as vocational curriculum has been accepted, the role of OLS in primary and even at the upper primary stage may not be seen as important or even acceptable by some. The arguments against would generally be the lack of maturity of the learners, lack of firmly acquired literacy-skills, etc. which would impede, self-learning. Also for working children, NFE has already been launched as an alternative facility for primary and middle-school education. But it must be pointed out that there are many older children and even literate adults who wish to take up further studies at the elementary level and for these, facilities of the OLS type must be provided.

Open elementary education could thus meet a genuine demand from clientele whose self-assessment, as protective learners would have to be accepted. The experience of NOS shows that such self-selected learners are highly motivated and perform well. This can happen with similar learners at the elementary stage. The proposed project of Open School in Andhra Pradesh, designed to cover learners from class VI onwards, provides concrete evidence that there is a perceived demand. The possibility of systematically organising OLS at the upper primary stage and thus bringing the bulk of drop-outs and push-outs of elementary schools back into education, needs to be explored. The Andhra Pradesh experiment is important from this standpoint. Projects of the type undertaken by Andhra Pradesh may be evolved in other States also, on the basis of local needs and possibilities.

The recommendations of the recent All-India Annual Conference of the Council of Boards of School Education (COBSE) held in Goa in November, 1991, are relevant in this respect. It was recommended that OLS should play an interventionist role in helping to achieve the national objective of 'Education for All', by providing a second chance and continuing education to the drop-outs, working-population, housewives and all deprived sections desirous of improving their educational qualifications, skills and training levels. It further recommended that State Open Schools may be set up, either as part of the Board in the initial stage, or as an independent agency.

Discrete subjects or clusters of certification-oriented subjects, viz. languages, sciences, mathematics, social sciences, etc. and vocation-oriented courses, depending on the learners' choice can be offered at the middle, secondary and higher secondary levels. The trend is already in evidence in programmes to propagate Hindi, Sanskrit, English, Mathematics, etc., through private channels.

2.5. OLS: VOCATIONAL SKILLS

Apart from academic open education, an encouraging trend is seen towards facilitating vocational education through the open system. Need-based courses related to self-employment and increased productivity are being evolved in the following areas:

(i) Agriculture: Farming, horticulture, floriculture, sericulture, agricultural technology, post harvest technology, food-processing, soil and water testing, livestock raising, marketing etc.

(ii) Engineering: Construction technology, construction-supervision, repair and maintenance of structures and of agricultural equipment, fabrication and

maintenance of electrical, mechanical and electronic equipment, etc.

(iii) *Health and sanitation*: Lab-technicians, paramedical personnel, water-analysts, malaria eradicators, vaccinators, creche-attendants, home-nursing and nutrition personnel;

(iv) *Services*: Secretarial courses, business management, accountancy, computer science, catering, journalism, textile design, interior decoration, garment-making, embroidery, etc. Depending on regional needs and demands, there could be special courses for preparing teachers and candidates for ministerial and other support-staff in government, trade and industry.

It is essential to build-up popular interest in open education, especially for turning the tide away from general academic education and guiding it towards vocational and lifeskill courses. For generating popular interest in vocational education and for exploding the myth that vocational education is meant for those having lower intelligence, Tamil Nadu prepared videos and exhibited them through several outlets including State TV Centres.

Popular interest in vocational centres at the middle and secondary stages was aroused with great success. Vocationalisation of secondary education has made remarkable progress in Tamil Nadu. Popularising and demystifying open education and especially open education for vocational skills must, therefore, be considered as an essential step in organising open education for employment generation.

2.6. OPEN EDUCATION: SUPPORT SYSTEM

2.6.1. Nodal Organisations

The nodal Ministry for implementing Open Education

will naturally be the Ministry of Human Resource Development, working in close collaboration with the Planning Commission in order to keep the programme geared to employment opportunities and lifelong learning for renewal of knowledge and skills. The National Open School and Indira Gandhi National Open University, along with State Open Schools and State Open Universities, would be the nodal agencies for organising, monitoring and evaluating various types of open education.

The experience of NOS in building course-linkages with Shramik Vidyapeeths for provision of vocational education and a similar approach by the YCMOU towards courses in horticulture, agriculture and related technology for rural learners are most welcome directions for the future of education in the rapidly changing socio-economic conditions in our country. The efforts of the YCMOU towards acquiring the character of a mass university as against the conventional concept that a university is meant for a few, are specially to be noted.

The highest policymaking and programme-evaluation organisation for education, with representatives from all the States, is the Central Advisory Board of Education (CABE). It may be beneficial to strengthen this role of the CABE further by enabling it to annually review national and international trends in education in the context of socio-economic and political factors, and advise government on new programme initiatives on the basis of a critical assessment of the situation. The CABE may also suggest, on the basis of evaluative reports, adaptation of the ongoing programmes in accordance with perceived needs. A Standing Committee of CABE on Open Education may be set up, as this would begin the trend towards looking upon education as a varied and selfrenewing system for stimulating social change and economic developments. With Member (Education),

Planning Commission, as Chairperson of this Committee, linkages between the HRD Ministry and Planning Commission would be facilitated, both at the policy and implementation levels.

2.6.2. Collaborative Agencies

Inter-ministerial collaboration appears to be crucial for achieving the objectives of open education. A wide-ranging spectrum of courses, catering to the needs of various sectors of the economy, would have to be offered and these can best be designed under the guidance of the Ministries concerned, viz. labour, health, agriculture, rural development, electronics, social welfare, communications, information and broadcasting, industries, co-operation, and human resource development.

The Ministries concerned would have to be systematically interlinked and their programmes coordinated from time to time. This collaboration will be essential in policy evolution, implementation, and sharing of financial allocations. Each concerned ministry may contribute a certain percentage of its budget towards supporting networked programmes of open education. In view of the complexity of this task of co-ordination it would be best to entrust it to the Planning Commission. Implementation of Open Education at the State and district levels has necessarily to be a collaborative effort by several agencies and institutions. Providing Learning Resource Centres, at the State and district levels Government and non-governmental agencies may be used for this purpose. For instance, SCERT, SIET, and (more recently) DIET exist in the government sector for servicing formal education. They have done it for such a long time, that it may be desirable to instil some flexibility in them by building their linkages with State

Resource Centres for Adult/Non-Formal Education, Shramik Vidyapeeths and Centres/institutions/ programmes conducted by voluntary agencies and other non-government organisations, for non-formal and part-time, own-time academic/vocational education.

The third level of collaboration will be with institutions and organisations that will act as Study Centres or Work Centres or workshops for learning and training. Today, there are over 10,000 vocational institutions which include vocational schools, vocational centres, community polytechnics, ITIs, Shramik Vidyapeeths, Krishi Vigyan Kendras, Health Centres, Farmers' Training Centres, training facilities offered by voluntary agencies, professional organisations, and so on.

Participation of competent and innovative organisations will have to be insisted upon at the State, District and local levels of which none will be subordinate to the other but will be treated as equally important for managing the flow of decisions and actions covering a purposive system of open education. It will have to be ensured that an innovation like open education does not get bogged down by administrative routines, and hierarchical official structures which impede the freedom of decisions and action at the point of delivery of services, and antiquated financial procedures which generally accompany conventional government schemes.

2.7. FINANCING OF OPEN EDUCATION

The collaboration of various organisations as envisaged in this Report would help optimise the use of existing resources and help larger and better returns at moderate cost. However, it must be remembered that while the initial investment in organising diversified Open Education has always been substantial on account of *(a)* preparation of multi-media learning packages, *(b)* the approximate period of about two years required to develop new courses and packages, and provision of some infrastructure.

However, the experience gained so far has proved beyond any doubt that the per student cost substantially decreases when the packages of teaching learning materials begin to be used by the learners for the courses in which they enrol. In the National Open School, using the usual formula of dividing the total expenditure on the programme by the total number of students, the current per student cost of imparting secondary education is found to be around Rs.200/- only. This covers both academic and vocational courses.

The YCMOU, which has just begun the programme with substantial packages of material (booklets, Audio Video Cassettes, gadgets for experiments, etc.) and linkages with numerous Contact Centres finds that the present per capita cost for newly instituted vocational courses is Rs.700/- but is expected to come down in the next 2 3 years as the coverage of the courses increases. It must also be noted that in the National Open School, no fees are charged to the prioritised client groups, viz. women, SC/ST, handicapped and ex-serviceman constituting about 60 per cent enrolment, while the general category pay moderate fees. In spite of this, restriction on income from fees, the NOS requires a government grant only to the extent of 15 per cent of its Non-Plan expenditure. Thus, the cost per student to be borne from government finances has remained quite low in the open education arrangements.

Any enterprise which gathers the utmost profit and human benefit from low financial investment but high efficiency in meeting a genuine demand, is to be preferred to a high-cost and low-return system.

Therefore, the open education system has to be seen from this angle also. In its practical side, jobs are done and items are produced as part of training. This aspect of production as a concomitant of training brings down the costs of open education still further. Although exact costing of the currently conducted courses is yet to be systematically done, the studies undertaken so far show that in open education, per student costs are about one-fourth of the costs in institutional education.

The cost-effectiveness of degree-level Distance Education which is the precursor of open education, is most impressive. At present, Distance Education accommodates nearly 12 per cent of the total enrolment at the tertiary level, while the size of allocation made by the UGC for this programme is only 0.5 per cent.. The establishment of more open universities for upgrading the correspondence courses of the traditional type, into contact-supported courses will no doubt require more initial investment. However, the quality of learning would greatly improve because of the well-designed packaged material and guidance provided by the Contact-Centres. Besides, when the student strength exceeds critical levels, the per capita costs of open higher education are expected to show much reduction.

The 11th Plan, which aims at removing educational disparities and increasing employment opportunities in non-traditional sectors to a large extent, recognises the need for updating the skills of many and imparting new skills to a vast number. Besides giving all children and youth the basic competence derived from general education, the objectives of the 11th Plan call for a new approach to educational organisation. Each State/UT may, therefore consider setting educational targets in accordance with its need for adult literacy, UPE/UEE, and education for wage-employment/self-employment. While an overall target for this goal can be broadly visualised at the national level, it is ultimately the UT/State and districtwise plans and targets that will spell out the organisational and financial implications of Open Education.

Considering the factors of unemployment and school-dropout as indicators for setting the targets for Open Education, the UT/State targets will have to be worked out accordingly. Skills, general information and social awareness of a level expected at the class VI-VIII level may be adequate as entry qualifications for those who wish to enter open education at the secondary level. Since many jobs and positions or further training stipulate a secondary level certificates, this stage may become the most acceptable to a large number of prospective learners.

2.8. EQUIVALENCE AND ACCREDITATION

It is a cardinal principle in OLS that the standard of curriculum and expected achievement in any of the open courses should not be less than that expected in an institutional course, although the contents may be somewhat different, being need-based. Comparability of standards is essential as the products of OLS would have to be acknowledged as equal to those expected to be produced by the institutional system. This is necessary to enable them to find placements in jobs or in higher education and to emphasise the concern for efficiency in studies and in work-performance. It is obvious that comparability or equivalence of open courses with institutional courses will have to be decided on the basis of carefully formulated criteria related to acquisition of expected competencies. An appropriate organisation will have to be entrusted with the task of formulation as well as application of the essential criteria of comparability. Considering that the open learning system is directed towards serving those who seek academic education as also those who seek job-oriented education, the evaluation organisation will have to be specially constituted.

IGNOU has already set-up a Distance Education Council for Higher Education. A similar Council for School Education is expected to evolve under the leadership of National Open School. There are privately conducted job-oriented open education institutions with direct linkages with market-demand and these use the demonstration of the expected levels of performance on the job, as the chief criterion of success. They do not bother about equivalence with the formal system.

A meeting ground for these diverse evaluation systems could be provided by a National Consortium on Open Education. Such a consortium could have representatives from the open system, formal system, business and industry, Planning Commission, Ministry of HRD, Ministry of Labour, NIEPA and specialists in social auditing, who can objectively consider the comparability and equivalence problems on the basis of evaluative studies and relevant research. In the meanwhile, criteria adopted by NOS and various open universities may prevail, with due Support from government because, ultimately, the open system has to prove its legitimacy and credibility through its performance which must be accepted both by the academic world and the world of work. The task of standardisation, accreditation and maintenance of quality will ultimately be performed by the National Consortium on Open Education which would also network and oversee the entire OLS in the country.

In relation to cost-benefit, accreditation and evaluation, some normative directions would be essential for OLS, as given below:

(*a*) Insistence on more intensive and more efficient use of existing facilities (buildings, equipment, software, curriculum, materials, training, orientation and experience). Systematic networking for better utilisation of resources.

(b) State Boards of (School) Education can easily provide infrastructural facilities, for parttime and own-time education. Similarly, institutions such as ITIs, Community Polytechnics, Krishi Vigyan Kendras, progressive farmers, small-scale industry, projects of voluntary agencies should participate in open education. The Community Polytechnics, KVKs and rural secondary and higher secondary schools, should play a wider and stronger role to support rural learners. Collaboration between The formal and the open learning channels should be carefully established so as to be mutually beneficial. For instance, some students of formal schools may find the distance education texts useful for improving their performance in the formal system. The multi-media packages may exert a beneficial effect on teaching-learning transactions in formal institutions. On the other hand, institutional facilities could be used for contact programmes in open education.

(c) Since open learning is essentially distance education which is a guided exercise in selflearning, a continuing effort to make the support institutions work efficiently must be made. A service orientation will be necessary for them. A narrowly commercial or quid pro quo attitude would be harmful to OLS.

(d) Financial support for students in OLS would have to be based on well-established criteria. Financial assistance to the State Open Schools would be necessary for programme-support such as, training, shared production of materials (print, audio and video packages), evaluation, and so on. The students should contribute to the services they receive, be it cost of materials, examination cost or student service cost, etc. No one should be made to lose self-respect by providing a totally free education, but reasonable concessions to the indigent and weak would be in order. It has been realised that whatever is free is seen as "worthless" by the recipients. The recipients gladly pay for whatever is worthwhile.

(e) The Open Learning organisation should have the necessary autonomy, with clear guidelines for operation. Old-fashioned administrative and financial controls based on the mistrust of the user should be discarded as they would obstruct the performance of the open learning system. OLS must remain dynamic. Autonomy coupled with accountability to the users, to society and to the norms of financial probity should be the way of functioning.

2.9. EXAMPLES OF OPEN EDUCATION IN INDIA

Five examples of Open Education are presented below. These indicate what can be achieved through OLS in relation to the educationally neglected segments of society. The examples are: NOS, APOS, IGNOU, YCMOU and Vivek Darpan.

2.9.1. National Open School

The National Open School already referred to, evolved out of the Open School of the Central Board of Secondary Education and has significant achievements to its credit. The number of students annually enrolled by it has increased from 3,164 in 1982-83 to 49,600 in 1989-90. In 1989-90, 6.4 per cent of the students were enrolled for the bridge course, 50.47 per cent for secondary courses and

43.31 per cent for Senior Secondary Courses. However, the new enrollment for the 'bridge courses' which are equivalent to the middle stage, has increased sharply from 7 per cent in 1982-83 to 24 per cent in 1987-88. This is significant since this post-primary group is the most educationally needy group. Despite English and Hindi as the only media of instruction, SC students accounted for 14.48 per cent and ST students accounted for 4.18 per cent in 1988-89. These percentages are well above the national averages. The majority of the students are in the age bracket 17 to 21. But it is noteworthy that those in the age group of 14 to 16 are 27.18 per cent which reveals the need for an alternative channel of middle-school education for young workers. In 1987-88, 15.04 of the students were employed and the rest i.e. 84.96 per cent were unemployed. In 1987-88, 20.7 per cent of the students were rural and the rest were urban.

As to the medium of instruction, 80 per cent of the students study through Hindi and the rest through English. The NOS offers a variety of courses but the foundation or basic education course is obligatory. Thereafter, nine secondary level courses, eighteen senior secondary level courses, two courses in community education, and seven vocational education courses offer a wide choice. The NOS works in a decentralised manner through "accredited institutions" of which there are 191 at present. Accredited institutions shoulder a variety of administrative responsibilities like distribution of prospectus, distribution of study materials and academic responsibility like `personal-contact' classes, evaluation of students' attainment, etc. However, there is a skeleton co-ordination centre for the North-East region based in Calcutta.

2.9.2. Open School in Andhra Pradesh

The Government of Andhra Pradesh has established, in

1991, an autonomous body called Andhra Pradesh Open School Society, to provide education for school dropouts especially girls, housewives and working women. The Society intends to cover 2.25 lakhs drop-outs in 10 districts of Andhra Pradesh, at the school stage. It will equip them with the competencies and qualifications necessary to become useful citizens, It will have general education courses from class V onwards with addition of courses like animal husbandry, agriculture, health and hygiene, rural based and agro-based technical courses. These will lead to certification. Life-enrichment courses without certification, will also be offered. The scheme is still in the formative stage and its funding is yet to be firmed up. However, since Andhra Pradesh was the first State to start Open Education at tertiary level in 1982, it has adequate experience in the area and its initiative at the elementary stage holds considerable promise to provide meaningful 'education for all' through the open channel.

2.9.3. Indira Gandhi National Open University (IGNOU)

IGNOU was established in 1985. It offers a variety of courses but its most Popular courses are Diploma in management which has an enrollment of 15148 students and non-formal Bachelor's Degree course with 26392 students. IGNOU has its own audio-video production studio. It has produced 169 video and 249 audio programmes to supplement printed material. For student services, it has an impressive network of 13 regional centres and 131 study centres throughout the country. By the end of 8th Plan, it proposes to establish a study centre in each district of the Country. IGNOU is also exploring the possibility of establishing study centres sponsored by industry and voluntary agencies. Mobile Study Centres for reaching remote areas are also planned. IGNOU is expected to have an enrolment of 2 lakh students at the end of the 8th Plan. (Proposed enrollment in March 1992: 1.50 lakhs). Apart from expanding the present certificate, diploma and graduate programmes in management, distance education, creative writing, commerce and library science, IGNOU is planning to offer courses in rural development, higher education and basic sciences in the near future. During the 8th Plan, IGNOU's thrust would be on introduction of non-traditional employment-oriented courses, courses in counselling and guidance for primary teachers, nutrition and health education, early childhood care and education, construction management and water resources management.

2.9.4. Yashwantrao Chavan Maharashtra Open University (YCMOU)

YCMOU, although formally established in 1989, had its antecedents in the Open Institution of the University of Poona under which a lot of preparatory work was done. The goal of the University is to become a "mass varsity". As such it emphasises vocational, technical and professional as well as general education programmes not only at the tertiary level but also at functional levels and outside the academic format, related to development and increased individual incomes.

YCMOU has planned courses in agriculture and horticulture. Ten representative crops have been selected, viz. Grapes, mangoes, cotton, groundnut, onion, 'toor' or 'arhar' (pigeon-pea), Kardi (safflower oil-seed), ber, (jujube), pomegranate and sugarcane. Working farmers study production processes with the help of specially written print materials, audio-visual aids, two-way communication between individual farmers and agriculture experts, and contact sessions. For contact sessions, the University uses the concept of "prayog parivaars" i.e. a sort of extended 'family' of 'experimenters' which enables producers/learners to get together to exchange ideas and benefit from each other's experience.

The Diploma in Applied Electronics developed by the University keeps in view the increasing demand for the trained electronics engineers, technicians and technical supervisors. Course-work consists of 16 credits (560 study hours) worth of theory, 16 credits worth of practical work and 8 credits worth of project work. Study materials have been developed by the best experts available in the field.

The University has undertaken to launch short-term certificate courses for various trades and professions. There would be no formal qualification necessary for entry to these programmes. At present 13 such courses are under preparation and would be launched in the near future.

In the development and implementation of its academic programmes, the YCMOU is extensively relying on the assistance of and contribution by experts from Universities, Colleges, Institutions and Organisations from all over the State. Some of these well-known organisations are: Yashwantrao Chavan Pratishthan, Mumbai, Homi Bhabha Centre for Science Education, Mumbai; Indian Institute of Technology (IIT) Mumbai; Maratha Chamber of Commerce, Pune; Maharashtra Grape Growers Association, Nashik; Marathwade University; and Poona University.

2.9.5. Vivek Darpan Project

Doubts about the utility of educational technology for and its Evaluation adult education have been set at rest with the findings of the evaluation study of the Vivek Darpan Project which was conducted on behalf of Department of Electronics by the Indian Institute of Mass

Communication (1991). The project selected 25 villages in each of the 4 districts (Aligarh in U.P., Bikaner in Rajasthan, Jhabua in MP and Ranchi in Bihar) which were provided with two Sanghamitra Community Video systems for Community Video Centres consisting of 20 CTV and VHS VCP. The back up software consisted of 660 different programme on 1/2 inch video cassettes. Two types of programmes motivational and local news type were generated locally for every Vivek Darpan Study Circle. ET & T was to provide two resident technicians for project maintenance, upkeep of hard ware and to maintain and organise "Circle Video Library". Two specially assigned officials were in charge of Central Programme Coordination. The specific objectives of the project were:

(i) To use the audiovisual media as a multi-user multi-tasking system for tackling wide-ranging needs of rural population.

(ii) To help in removing illiteracy and to give the literate the vocational and various forms of guidance for improvement in the quality of life.

(iii) To motivate the illiterates to move towards literacy by making them aware of the usefulness of literacy.

(iv) To create an experimental infrastructure to evaluate the various types of video programmes for future replicability.

(v) To evaluate field performance of hardware.

The evaluation showed that the project effectively did not take off in Ranchi. In the remaining three districts, the project faced a lot of technical difficulties including maintenance of TV sets.

The examples cited above differ considerably in their conceptualisation, content and details of implementation. But all of them focus on the neglected sections of society in order to increase their competence as citizens, students and producers of economic benefits. Besides, each example recognises the need to provide localised, client-specific, education programmes, with a built-in provision for experimentation, evaluation and safeguards for protecting the qualitative aspects of the programme. The principle that standards of human competence are not static and uniform but ever-evolving and multiform, is also implicit in these examples.

2.10. FUTURE OF OLS IN INDIA

OLS has a tremendous potential for the fulfilment of the objectives of 'Education for All', vocationalisation of secondary education, training and retraining for wage-employment and self-employment of the rural population and urban workers, along with academic advancement of learners, in accordance with their requirements. Open education, therefore, can play a significant role in spreading relevant education in a big way and help gear up rural and urban economies by increasing productivity.

The National Open School, already established, would have to be strengthened for meeting the educational needs of *(a)* Open Secondary Education *(b)* Open Higher Secondary Education, *(c)* Open Vocational Education and *(d)* Open Upper Primary education, the last on an experimental basis. Focus on out-of-school urban, rural and tribal youth, adolscent girls, women, and the rural farming communities in general is essential for linkages between education and development.

State Boards of Secondary/Higher Secondary Education have accepted the need for an open channel of education. Each State/UT may be required to set targets in accordance with needs, available facilities and facilities to be newly provided.

At present, there is a National Open University (IGNOU) and four State Open Universities. Some more may come up in the near future. Massoriented State Universities like Yashwant Rao Chavan Maharashtra Open University, Nashik (YCMOU), have already started well-designed courses for locale-specific agricultural / horticultural education in specific market oriented produce like oil-seeds, pulses, grapes, mangoes, etc. The existing Open Universities may consider innovative programmes on the lines of YCMOU for accelerating the pace of rural productivity in their region.

The Shramik Vidyapeeths under the Department of Education have been imparting skill-improvement training and life-skills to urban industrial workers in the organised sector and their families. To the extent possible, SVPs have also been giving market-oriented job-training to youth and women in the needy urban groups. In the 8th Plan the Shramik Vidyapeeths should be guided to shift their attention much more to the organisation of self-employment training for youth and women in the urban informal sector, relating to technical skills, marketable arts and crafts, urban services, and so on.

Business, industry and professional organisations may be called upon to set up their own Education and Training Units with a view to training, in collaboration with open education institutions, the manpower required according to their own emerging demands. The Chambers of Commerce and professional organisations like Builders' Association, Engineers' Association, etc., should be encouraged to interact with educational institutions at various stages to provide job-oriented training in keeping with market demand. Their course-materials and techniques of training may be guided by Open Universities and Open School Organisations, under appropriate contracts.

Various Ministries involved with imparting training and providing sectorwise manpower need to interact and build linkages for evolving open education and training programmes. These programmes would need standardisation, modularisation an gradation so as to ensure their efficiency and market acceptability. Eventually, they should aim at getting accrediation for which organisational arrangements would have to be made. Each Ministry may contribute from its budget an appropriate percentage for this purpose to the Open School/ Open University selected as collaborator. In view of the complexity of the task of coordination, it is best to entrust it to the Planning Commission.

The design and development of a variety of location-specific courses bearing on agricultural, agro-based industries and related services such as processing, storage, transport, marketing, accounting and so on may be looked upon as an essential aspect of micro-planning for area-development. Agricultural Universities in collaboration with Open School and Open University structures should undertake this activity and build practice-networks through Krishi Vigyan Kendras, Community Polytechnics, other Rural Development Organisations and Programmes such as KVIC, Khadi and Village Industries Boards, TRYSEM and so on. DRDA's should be involved in this programme.

Resources and cooperation of voluntary organisations may be enlisted for extension of the Open Education Channels especially for employment oriented courses in health and sanitation, agriculture, horticulture, livestock development, artisanship, construction sector, etc.

There should be a large OLS teacher training programme, especially for meeting the urgent requirements for trained primary and secondary teachers in the predominantly tribal education programme of the North-Eastern States. Also, teachers at all levels including instruction in AE/NFE programme should be required to understand the need, purposes and processes of OLS.

IGNOU and NOS may prepare a programme for the induction training of teachers in remote geographical areas where the need is most urgent.

The possibility of establishing a dedicated TV channel for education aimed to benefit the clientele identified in this Report (Girls, Women, SC/ST, Rural and Urban Poor, Unemployed Youth and so on), as recommended by the Working Group on Satellite Services for Education, should be seriously explored.

Since the Open Learning System consists of a cluster of innovations as regards planning, management, financing, networking, contact-centres, packaged materials containing both print and electronic media, localised supervision of implementation and achievement effort through Education Complexes, use of the dialectic method of teaching-learning incorporating the basic principles of andragogy, community Support and so on, all the personnel engaged in the planning and process of these varied innovations would require intensive training. These training programmes should be planned and organised by the NOS, IGNOU, YCMOU and other organisations who have acquired the capability of launching and managing educational innovation and change. Adequate financial support for this programme would have to be provided without delay, by pooling the financial resources of government and interested agencies.

3

Open Schooling in India

Open learning can be defined as an approach to learning that gives students flexibility and choice over what, when, at what pace, where, and how they learn. It serves as a source of education for the marginalised and disadvantaged sectors of the society, besides being desirable due to its innate relation with human psyche and psychological development. Its benefactors include the physically and mentally handicapped, the female population, school dropouts, residents of rural areas and remote regions.

Open schooling is also preferred by students pursuing careers, which require them to devote more time than what the stringent formal school systems with its time-bound structure and attendance compulsions can permit. Students who wish to choose specific combinations of subjects, which may not be possible under the formal system, also turn to open schools. The system also contributes to the cause of adult literacy.

3.1. ORIGIN OF OPEN SCHOOLING IN INDIA

A person is considered literate if he or she can both read and write with understanding. Attaining higher rates of literacy in this basic form topped the list of educational concerns for the government in the past several decades.

Schemes like the National Literacy Mission, Universalisation of Elementary Education, Sarva Shikha Abhiyan (SSA) and other related government schemes have accrued to the increase in numbers of people receiving primary education/basic literacy.

Besides catering to the 'high-school' population of students, it was also important to find a way of making secondary education viable for those who for one reason or the other could not attend regular school. It was important to give students who dropped out of school a chance to complete their education, especially looking at the marginal decline in the percentage of dropouts (from classes I-X) from 69.6 per cent in 1995-96 to only 61.92 per cent in 2004-05. To reduce the number of dropouts and to attract more of them to complete their education, there was a need to bring in the option of skill-based learning or vocational education at secondary and senior secondary levels.

Equally substantial was the need to target the adult population of the country, with the adult illiteracy rates being as high as 39 per cent according to the 2001 census. Attending regular school classes from morning till afternoon daily was not a feasible option for full-time or part-time workers. Giving them independence from the time-bound concept of studying followed by the formal system was utterly essential.

There was a need to make higher education an option for people even for those who didn't have schools in their vicinity. Many stopped sending their daughters to school because they considered it dangerous for them to travel large distances to reach school. Female dropout rates, female illiteracy rates are much higher than those of their male counterparts. Women, after getting married early, had very little option of continuing their studies even if they wanted to. Hence a relaxed system in terms of time constraints was a much-welcomed respite from the inflexible formal system. To encourage people from economically backward sections of the society to participate, the fee structure also had to be kept low.

Considering such grave needs for an alternative to the formal system of education, the open schooling system was introduced in India.

The advent of Open Schooling in India was through the CBSE initiated Open School Project in 1979. A decade later, in the year 1989, the Ministry of Human Resource and Development set up an autonomous organisation that took charge of the project and the new institution was named National Open School (NOS). The NOS was renamed as National Institute of Open Schooling (NIOS) in 2002. Hence, NIOS evolved from an off-branch of the Central Board of Secondary Education, from an institution serving about 40,000 to the largest open school in the world, which enrolled 2,90,983 students in the year 2006-2007 and was serving a total of 14,27,000, according to the figures given.

Because of the 'open' or 'learner dependent' nature of open learning, it is classified as a non-formal mode of education. The formal mode of education, on the contrary, is the system followed by schools, where the learning is monitored by the school curriculum, which depends on the board it is affiliated to. These schools are normally affiliated to one of following boards:

- Central Board of Secondary Education (CBSE).
- Council for the Indian School Certificate Examination (CISCE).
- State Boards of the state where the school is located.

Under British Rule, the Indian education system went through various stages of development. Back in 1921, the 'UP Board of High School and Intermediate Education' was the first board to be set up, which was later centralised in 1929 and given the name 'Board of High School and Intermediate Education, Rajputana'.

Despite the centralisation of this institution of education, various regions preferred education systems to have regional jurisdictions and often even have the regional languages as the medium of instruction. In order to cater to the region specific needs of students, State Boards came up in certain states. In 1952, the left out regions were also included in the jurisdiction of Board of High School and Intermediate Education, Rajputana and hence evolved the Central Board of Secondary Education with 8998 schools affiliated to it as on July 2, 2007.

Meanwhile, the Anglo-Indian community residing in India had a special Inter-State Board for Anglo-Indian Education, which was affiliated with the University of Cambridge, Local Examination Syndicate (i.e. the examinations conducted were based on the study material provided by the Local Examination Syndicate, Cambridge). In 1958, an Indian council moulded the syllabi as per the needs of the country and took control of the education and examination procedures there after. This council, 'Council for the Indian School Certificate Examination', over time not only catered to the Anglo-Indian community but also started having public schools seeking affiliation.

The CBSE, CISCE and NIOS come directly under the Ministry of Human Resource Development as boards of secondary education, while State Boards fall under the Education Ministries of the concerned state.

3.2. THE NATIONAL OPEN SCHOOL (NOS)

The National Open School was established in November 1989 with a mission of providing 'education for all', 'greater equity and justice in the society', and 'the evolution of a Learning Society'. The objectives of the NOS were stated as follows:

– To provide opportunities for continuing and developmental education to interested learners through courses and programmes of general education life enrichment modules and vocational courses up to pre degree level,

– To provide consultancy services and to engage in model building in close collaboration with states and variety of other agencies or institutions,

– To serve as an agency for effective dissemination of information related to distance education and open learning,

– To identify and promote standards of learning in distance education systems and open schools which may be set up in different parts of the country, through research and evaluation and to maintain standards of equivalence with the formal system, while keeping its own distinct character.

It is the largest open schooling system in the World. Its client groups include the girls, the women, the Scheduled Castes, the Scheduled Tribes, the rural people, the urban poor, the unemployed, the part by employed, the under employed, the young and the adult, the partially handicapped etc. The NOS has more than 1000 study centres located in the territory of India and it also has five centres outside the country. The cumulative enrolment of the student exceeds over half a million. The annual enrolment trend shows a steady growth and in the current year the enrolment at secondary and senior secondary level alone is expected over 150 thousand.

The NOS runs programmes at the elementary, secondary and senior secondary levels in academic and vocational streams. The courses are taken as a part of the requirement of certification or even as 'stand alone' courses. The vocational courses are often taken as stand alone courses. These range from cutting and tailoring to computer applications. Again, the NOS run various life enrichment programmes intended particularly towards improving the quality of life. These learners are reached through the Accredited Institutions (AIs) or Accredited Vocational Institutions (AVIs) where the contact programmes are held. The contact programmes are primarily related to the teaching of the courses and conduct of the practical. There are some major lacunae in the transaction of these teaching learning strategies which is a cause of concern to the NOS.

3.2.1. Functioning of NIOS

3.2.1.1. Courses Offered

The NIOS offers courses under:

1. Open Basic Education Programmes (OBEs):
   (a) OBE-A level (equivalent to class III),
   (b) OBE-B level (equivalent to class V), and
   (c) OBE-C level (equivalent to class VIII),
2. Secondary Education Course (equivalent to Class X).
3. Senior Secondary Education Course (equivalent to Class XII).
4. Life Enrichment Courses.
5. Vocational Education Courses.

3.2.1.2. Admission

Accredited Institutions

Distance education causes a 'disconnect' between learners and the institution of learning. Certain institutions (schools or NGOs satisfying certain conditions) affiliate themselves to the National Institute of Open Schooling and serve as the student interface. These study centres are classified as:

1. Accredited Institutions (AIs).
2. Accredited Vocational Institutes (AVIs).
3. Special Accredited Institutions for the Education of the Disadvantaged (SAIEDs).

It is at these study centres that all transactions between NIOS and the learners take place. The forms can be purchased and submitted here along with the fees. NIOS study material is delivered to these centres and thereafter collected by students. While admission for the Vocational Courses is open throughout the year, that to Academic Courses is open only for a specified period of time. The fee to Secondary Courses is under Rs.1000 while that for Senior Secondary Education is under Rs.1200. There are special concessions for girls, SC/ST, ex-servicemen, differently-abled persons.

Personal Contact Programme (PCP)

Each accredited institution is supposed to organise Personal Contact Programmes on weekends and holidays under the guidance of a facilitator, who is generally a scholar associated with the NIOS. During these sessions, teachers (teachers of the school if the school itself is a study centre, or those of a school working in collaboration with the study centre if it is an NGO) help students with the course work. Special practical classes are also held for the students who take up courses that require the same. These institutions also have to carry out motivational sessions for the enrolled students, to keep them enthusiastic about the course. Tutor Marked Assignments (TMA). Each student has to submit three assignments in each subject taken up by him/her. These are corrected by the teacher teaching that subject at the accredited institution (if the AI itself is the school) or at a school associated to the accredited institution. The final grades have to be sent to NIOS before the student appears for the final exam, and the better two out of three are counted with the total score.

3.2.1.3. *Syllabi*

The NIOS has its own scholars prepare the study material for various academic and vocational courses that it offers. This material is available in English, Hindi and Urdu medium. They use the National Curriculum Framework, as designed by NCERT, as a source of reference. The study material is designed in a self-explanatory way and it comprises of books, and may include Audio-cassettes and videocassettes also. They also use televised mediums like the Doordarshan and the Radio to broadcast study programmes.

3.2.1.4. *Examinations*

Examinations are held twice a year, once in April-May period and then again in October-November. These examinations are conducted with government schools, Kendriya Vidyalayas, Navodaya Vidyalayas and some accredited institutions as centres. NIOS also extends to students the facility of taking exam at anytime of the year when they feel prepared, in case seats are available in that examination. This facility can be availed at an additional cost of Rs. 25. A student is allowed to appear for an exam. in the same subject as many as nine times in a time span of five years. He/she is allowed one attempt to retake an exam to improve the score, but the fee for that subject has to be paid again. NIOS follows the system of 'credit accumulation' (i.e. credits are added up till the student finally passes the exams in all subjects of a course).

In case a student fails to qualify a course but passes in at least one subject of the course, then he/she can take the open school examination for the rest of the subjects (provided these subjects are offered by the NIOS). In the process, credits from at most two subjects, which he/ she had already passed, can be transferred to NIOS and he would be exempted from giving those papers again. This is done at a cost of Rs. 75 per paper.

3.2.1.5. Functioning of CBSE and CISCE

The CBSE, CISCE and the State Boards function along very similar lines. The following is a brief description of how this happens:

Admission

They operate through institutions, which affiliate themselves to the board. An institution can get affiliated to one of the above boards if it satisfies certain conditions, as decided by the respective board, emphasis is laid on the infrastructure, medium of instruction, minimum qualification of teachers, fees charged, conducting examinations and keeping records. Once affiliated, an institution can commence its functioning as a school, based on the guidelines of that board. The admission of students into any of the boards happens through schools affiliated to them. Hence, the curriculum of the school is imposed upon the students. Both CBSE and CISCE follow minimum and maximum age bars imposed by the state in which the affiliated school is situated.

Cources

Each board has a set of subjects that it offers for every class and a list of recommended books for the same. At

Secondary and Senior Secondary levels when students have an option of choosing subjects they want to study, it varies from school to school what combinations can be offered. This depends on the availability of teachers, classrooms, time constraints and few other factors depending on the school. Only those subjects in which regular classes are held at the schools can be taken up by students. While CBSE allows students to take an additional subject at both Secondary and Senior Secondary levels if the school at which they're studying has a department for that subject even if he/she does not attend regular classes in the same.

Syllabi

The CBSE syllabi for classes I through VIII are chosen by the school authorities and mandatory verification of the middle school syllabus is required by the board. While for the CISCE, for classes below class IX, the syllabus affiliated to the State Government is followed. Syllabi for CBSE are prepared normally by the National Council of Educational Research and Training (NCERT), while those of the CISCE are put together by the Research, Development and Consultancy Division of the board. Different state boards have different reference standards for setting their syllabi.

Examination

CBSE and CISCE conduct national level exams for classes X and XII only. For the lower grades, the affiliated schools conduct exams. It is the schools that decide the frequency and syllabus of the examinations that they conduct. State Boards conduct state level annual exams for certain classes differing from state to state. The system followed for the remaining classes is same as that of the CBSE or CISCE. The fees charged by CBSE for the board exam at All India level is Rs. 300-350, while the same for CISCE is about Rs. 500. But students have to an annual school fees too, which varies from school to school.

3.2.2. Special Features of NIOS

1. The lenient time constraint of five years given to students to clear each of the Secondary and Senior Secondary (with either or both Academic or Vocational courses) with as many as nine possible attempts, makes it much easier for students with:
   - Learning disabilities.
   - Physical handicaps.

   to take exams. and even do well as compared to their probable performance under the formal system of education. It also has the provision of readmission after 5 years.
2. NIOS gives the student freedom to choose when they want to study and does not keep them time-bound as is the case with the formal systems. Hence, it is a feasible option for:
   - People engaged in part-time or full time jobs.
   - House-wives.
   - Students who would like to pursue a personal extra-curricular interest as a profession.
3. Chained by societal norms or bound by family responsibilities, it serves as a lucrative option for the female population. They don't even have to travel to school and can learn from home itself. Similar is the case in regions where no schools can be built in the vicinity and in rural areas. The NIOS has even used media through Doordarshan and radio broadcasts to reach the rural population of the country.

4. Because it has no age bar and is very lenient on the numbers of attempts a student is allowed, NIOS gives a chance to school drop-outs (even adults) to continue with studies.
5. As observed by a developmental worker, "Street children, child workers and child prostitutes who have been rehabilitated cannot cope with formal education." Hence open schooling comes handy.
6. NIOS allows students at Secondary and Senior Secondary level to take up any combination of subjects from those it offers in both academic and vocational fields. This may not be possible through schools because of the unavailability of teachers in particular subjects.
7. A student can take admission into just one or two subjects at any level and get a mark sheet (not certificate) for the same on passing the examination, without having to do the whole course. This is called 'Part Admission'. Though the CISCE also allows students to do the same at Senior Secondary level, but for this, the student has to pass their old school's final exam. for class XI in the same subject. Only then in the subsequent year is he/she eligible to appear for the class XII exam in the same. Though unlike the NIOS, these candidates cannot appear as individual candidates, and can only go through the school where they passed class XI and XII from.
8. A student can branch out of the normal academic programme and take up vocational courses after class V, VIII, X or XII depending on the basic qualifications required to learn the skill. For instance, a student can choose a vocational course like 'House Wiring and Electrical Appliance Repairing' after clearing class V exams or 'House Keeping' after passing class X.

9. NIOS offers students the option of choosing one or two subjects extra, i.e. in addition to those chosen by them at Secondary or Senior Secondary level. Though under CBSE, a student can take up a sixth subject, besides the basic 5 if the school has a department for the same irrespective of whether the school can hold classes in the same or not. CISCE allows 7 subjects, all of which have to be regularly taught at school, though the pass certificate is given even if the student passes any 6 out of the 7.

3.2.3. Enrolment

The policy of open schooling is the bridge between India today and an India with 100 per cent literacy. The syllabus of CBSE and NIOS is based on the same reference structure compiled by NCERT called the National Curriculum Framework. As observed by the principal of a CISCE school, the syllabus followed by NIOS is comparable to that followed by CISCE or any other national board. Hence, open schooling in theory seems to be reaching where the formal system cannot reach, while maintaining the quality of education. But as is the case with many policies, there is a stark contrast between the policy of open schooling in theory and in reality. It is far from being implemented the way its makers may have wanted it to be. Despite having completed almost two decades as an autonomous board of education at national level, the pass rates for academic courses at both Secondary and Senior Secondary levels have been stuck in the late 20s and early 30s, when those of their counter parts (CBSE, CISCE) are consistently maintained in late 80s and early 90s.

NIOS does not keep any record of the number of candidates based on economic status or categorised by the reason for joining open school Clearly, the low pass rates have a major contribution from the general category. Hence, very little light can be thrown on what the reason for such low pass rates is. But it does raise a question about the quality of education or at least the comprehensibility of study material.

When analysing the age-wise enrolment of students by NIOS, almost 74 per cent students are from the age group of 15-20 years, indicating that it has not been very successful in serving the adult population of the country. A similar argument can be put forward from the gender point of view. Gender–wise enrolment of students, as in the following figure shows that every year, the number of females enrolled is less than half of the males enrolled in the same year, challenging the success of NIOS in enabling women to continue education at secondary level. This is despite the fact that one of its target sectors is the female population of the country. Even the total enrolment, from the above figure, does not show a consistent increase.

Table 3.1. Age-wise Enrolment of Students in 2006-07

Age	Range No of learners
10-14	10873
15-20	215233
21-25	43022
26-30	11642
31-35	5122
36-40	2864
41-45	1394
46-50	648
51-55	153
56-60	22
61-65	4
66-70	2
71-75	0
76-80	4
Total	290983

Table 3.2. Category-wise Enrolment of Students in 2006-07

Category	Academic	%
General	231334	79.50
SC	36599	12.58
ST	21029	7.23
Ex-Servicemen	434	0.15
Handicapped	1587	0.55
Total	290983	100.00

Table 3.3. Gender-wise Enrolment of Students (2001-2006)

Year	Male	Female	Total
2006-07	199788	91195	290983
2005-06	182440	84586	267026
2004-05	162351	75718	238069
2003-04	220103	100907	321010
2002-03	164550	113684	278234
2001-02	152286	62296	214582

An NIOS co-ordinator, at the condition of being kept anonymous, elaborated on the delay in arrival of study material and even funds for Personal Contact Programmes at their study centre. There have been complains about discrepancies between questions asked in the exams and the syllabus. All these factors place NIOS secondary to formal system of education. Only a single conclusion can be drawn from the above reasoning: the concept of open schooling is an excellent alternative to the formal system in theory. But it is presently only a substitute to the formal system and has to go a long way in being implemented ideally enough to graduate from its present status to being an alternative to the formal system.

3.3. PROBLEMS IN OPEN SCHOOLING

The problems that we face are with regard to reaching

the unreached in the nook and corner of the country. The access of these unreached to the media is a question mark. While the television is the most effective media to reach them, its logistics are fraught with problems that are not generally appreciated in very many countries. For instance the power shortage in the town and villages is chronic problem. Many a times it is just not available for days together. The Internet facilities are purely urban phenomena and are not available to the type of clientele that we seek to reach.

The best bet so far is to depend on the print media and we depend on the newspaper, both national and local, English, Hindi and local languages to reach our messages. Then we depend almost entirely on the print media to impart our courses, which again are distributed through our AIs. AI s being strategically located from the point of view of reach and infrastructure facilities become the hub for contact and reaching these learners.

We have not reached a stage of media development where we could reach our learners individually through Internet or Internet chatting. Therefore, we have to work in two stages. First, building and updating the capacities at the National level through our Human Resource development at the NOS level building the capacity at the Contact Centre level. The first is rather easy because of availability of expertise and technology at the national level, while at the second level i.e. at the AI level, the logistics of reaching them is problematic. Any cascade model of training has its own inherent shortcoming. The transfer loss in such a training model is of no mean magnitude.

In order to reach these AIs we have tried the video-conferencing technology with two way audio and one way video technique. Due to limited down linking facilities this has remained an experimental exercise and has not been used as a normal and regular mode of interaction. So far, we have to reach the AI s in advance through mail to intimate them of the programme, arrange for their assembly at the appointed day and time at a place where the video conferencing and Subscriber Trunk Dialing (STD) facilities are available and then make them participate in the process. It also involves, though only at the initial stages, removal of the inhibitions and fear of the advanced technology.

3.4. CURRENT TRENDS

Largely we are dependent on the written materials. We announce our programmes through the press, issue guidelines to the AIs through letters, booklets and circulars. Admission and examination matters are handled at the AI level. We used the video conferencing for the training of the AI personnel, mainly coordinators, on an experimental basis just last year and propose to undertake this year also. But we have to depend on the facilities available at other sister institution. The contents and time of such conferencing is under revision and the tutors at the AI s are also proposed to be included. We are working towards including the pedagogy of how to anticipate and diagnose the learning knots of the individual learner and how to solve them. Individualised instruction will be given centre stage in the teaching learning methodology. In other words, diagnostic and remedial approach coupled with individualised learning would be the package to be transacted through this mode.

With the dedicated education satellite coming into operation recently we are producing video lessons to be telecast for the benefit of the learners directly, provided, of course, the learners have access to it. These telecast are in the morning with a repeat in the evening. It can be seen that we are working at different levels and using appropriate technology to deliver our lessons and achieving our mission.

3.5. FUTURE DIRECTIONS

The NOS has a plan of extensive use of technology in the coming years. It is at work to develop parallel test items for each level of examination conducted by it. These items will be fed into the computer and it will be possible to generate innumerable sets of parallel tests. Necessary software will be developed for this purpose. Thus with the available technology it may be possible for us to reach a stage of 'examination on demand' without the fear of copying or mass copying plaguing the examination system currently. Similarly a situation of admission on demand is also envisaged.

Taking into account the fact that India is a multilingual society with pluralistic culture, it is necessary that the entire education should be locally relevant. The need for decentralisation is of utmost importance. The NOS is moving towards this goal by having ten regional offices (it already has eight). These eight regional offices are connected through fax but soon will have Internet facilities. Thus we may obviate the need of wide area networking. Then these regional centres will be working as extended outreach stations of the NOS for the AI s Decentralisation, therefore, is the prime need of this country, particularly because of its size, variety of its culture, flora and fauna. Contextually, the issue of the relevance has been at a discount for quite a long time and has created certain aberration in Indian education. This needs to be corrected by allowing greater flexibility in curriculum development and implementation. Even the States in India are too big a unit for that matter. The promotion of establishment of the State Open Schools is one of the priority areas of concern to the NOS.

4

State Open Universities

For long, Distance Education (DE) was regarded as a poor cousin of the school and university system and the products from this stream were considered as "second class citizens" in the realm of academia and society at large. The pioneering and excellent efforts by the UK Open University have largely served to neutralise this concept and accord a respectable status to Open and Distance Learning (ODL). The model of this university in fact became the basis for the establishment and administration of many open universities in different parts of the world including India.

With the advent of Information Technology (IT) and the consequent networking of even remote regions on this planet, young and old learners everywhere have ample opportunities to equip themselves with knowledge and skills. There is, of course, the essential condition for educational institutions at every level to create the infrastructure. It is here that wide variations are found in a country like India where a large talent pool exists without the requisite science and technology (S&T) support in many parts of the country. Even in the places where a modicum of such S&T support is available, the mindset of the staff in charge unfortunately is not tuned towards taking things forward. This is not to say that these variations depict a bleak picture. Far from it, there are bright patches as well.

4.1. DEVELOPMENT OF STATE OPEN UNIVERSITIES

The setting up of the Andhra Pradesh Open University (now called Dr. B.R.Ambedkar Open University or BRAOU) in 1982 marked a milestone in the annals of ODL in India. Remarkable progress in the development of the university could be noted in the first decade and a half. This covered areas like staff recruitment and training, networking and partnerships through the use of technology, science education and induction of innovative practices. Also, the production of audio and video lessons received a stimulus.

Yet, the deficiencies due to lack of physical facilities in study centres came in the way of larger number of students making use of the material. On the whole, it can be said that the dynamic leadership during the early years paved the way for further development. The establishment of Prof.G.Ram Reddy Academy of Distance Education (GRADE) served to stimulate research in ODL. It is unfortunate, however, that in the last few years, a situation of complacency has taken hold of the people in charge of the OU and bureaucratic control dominates. The campus and building along with infrastructure facilities are, however, quite impressive but red tapism is a worrying factor.

What keeps the BRAOU going is the dedicated team of competent academics. Celebrating its Silver Jubilee, BRAOU successfully organised recently an International Conference on Open and Distance Education.

The years 1987 to 1998 witnessed the creation of eight state Open Universities, namely Bihar (1987), Rajasthan (1987), Maharashtra (1989), Madhya Pradesh (1991),

Gujarat (1994), Karnataka (1996), W. Bengal (1997), and Uttar Pradesh (1998). Tamil Nadu came up with its own OU in 2002 but good design of special programmes like livelihood education is already on. Of the nine SOUs mentioned above, YCMOU in Maharashtra and NSOU in West Bengal have registered remarkable progress, the former going far in giving a thrust to agriculture education and practices. The others reveal several minor variations in matters of disciplines of study anddelivery of courses. Except for the initial euphoria at the time of inauguration, nothing much by way of sustaining programmes seems to be in evidence in the case of a few SOUs.

On the national scene, one should mention the efforts that are being made to integrate the several components of learning with the help of information technology. Curriculum design, evaluation of assignments from the learners, student support services, and examination schedule are all being brought into this web by dedicated personnel. But alas, these efforts seem to be somewhat thwarted by lack of support or apathy from the levels above. Among the multitude of reasons for this sad state of affairs must be listed interpersonal relations, jealousy and beaurocratic ineptitude.

All over the world, people are familiar with red tapism in the government offices and machinery. But in India, this negative trait seems to have made heavy inroads in the university and academic circles. This seems to be especially relevant in the case of India's state open universities where the academic leaders are expected to give a thrust to development of the learning system and make it vibrant and exciting. A crucial reason for the variability in the development of the State Open Universities in the country may be taken as this one.

These are only a few of the areas where a lot of improvement is called for. No doubt, dealing with large numbers of students in a variety of disciplines is difficult but this is what the Open Universities are supposed to do efficiently and earnestly so that society ultimately gets the benefit. The learners cannot be taken for granted and their innate desire to acquire knowledge and skills must be respected. Whether all the existing Open Universities in India manage to accomplish the avowed objective of their establishment is unfortunately open to question. Granting that difficult barriers exist one has a feeling that the performance in many cases could have been better.

The National Education Policy (NEP-1986) and the subsequent Programme of Action (POA) can be considered as two outstanding documents in the field of education. They covered almost all vital segments relating to education, science and technology, training of manpower etc. In fact, the NEP urged that every State in India must set up an Open University in order to provide access to the ever increasing numbers of aspirants for higher education. But what is the situation today?

Only 13 States out of 29 have established Open Universities, there of them only recently. (Out of the three, Uttranchal, now called Uttarakhand and Chhatisgarh were carved out of then existing larger States, thanks to political compulsions.) and Assam became a late entrant. In spite of the push from above, several states have not set up Open Universities as envisaged in the NEP. This provides a clue to the functioning of the education system as a whole. The commitment from the political powers that be is not much in evidence in spite of the rhetoric flowing from the platforms.

Even where the Open Universities were setup, it looks as if there were compelling extraneous reasons for the act on the part of state governments. This bring us down to the question of institutional leadership. Here, the appointment of vice chancellors assumes a vital role.

The V.C. as a leader must be a person of impeccable integrity and imbued with a spirit of total dedication to the cause of open and distance learning. Only then, reasonable progress in the path of development of ODL can be made. Much depends on the leadership from above and the Vice Chancellor must be a person owing allegiance to the cause of scholarship and learning, not to any political power. Otherwise, how can one expect the Open University to become "a learning community based on reflective practice"? In the same breath, how can one expect the academic and non-academic staff to have "total commitment to institutional vision and plan"? Or for that matter, will it be possible to recruit and nurture "academic faculty with high academic integrity and a commitment to research"?

With sixteen recognised regional languages and over 1600 dialects and spoken languages, India faces formidable challenges in making higher education available to the lower down strata of society. Really good teaching material, if it undergoes transcreation from one language to another, can reach larger numbers of learners. In a way this also may be taken as a creative activity, almost like fresh writing on the subject. In the Open University system, the content creator, editor and media producer play a crucial role in transforming even a drab subject into an exciting one, able to rivet the attention of the learner.

Course writing and development is as much valuable as scripting for audio-video programmes. There are other aspects requiring attention from the faculty, administrative staff and technical personnel engaged in the production of material. Indeed, in the open university system, the teachers are willy nilly made to perform several roles. The academic faculty posted to Open University from the traditional or conventional institutions has to adjust to this regimen so that the Open

University system works fairly smoothly. It is here that the importance of periodical training of staff and refresher programmes for them gains in value.

Experts and keen observers of the higher education scene have been quick to draw comparisons between the distance teaching institutions like open universities and their conventional or traditional counterparts. The Open University system especially is forced to make course delivery through different channels like audio, video and now internet in contrast to the face-to-face teaching-learning process common in the traditional university. In the latter, eminent and gifted teachers have succeeded in sparking the interest of generations of students whereas in the open university system what counts is the course material and packages with intrinsically high academic merit. Thus, there is a vital need to expose the faculty to modern developments in the design and preparation of courses. The State Open Universities in India do not present a uniformly satisfactory picture when it comes to this area also.

Some peculiar features pertaining to the state open universities in India deserve to be noted. These include:

1. These higher education institutions trying to duplicate courses offered by traditional universities (B.A., B.Sc., B.Com etc. in the undergraduate level and M.A., M.Com etc. at the postgraduate level)
2. Hesitancy to experiment with latest technological tools for the broadcasting of courses and lessons.
3. Funding from government sources tapering off and greater dependence of open universities on resources generated by themselves.
4. Larger drop-out rates despite a reasonably long time frame.

It has to be noted that the Indian government had made known its desire to cut down expenditure on higher education stating that universalisation of primary/ elementary education is far more important for a developing country. Here again, bright patches emerge in the case of open universities with good leadership at the top and a congenial environment for work. Vice chancellors with vision and belief in long range planning have brought about certain desirable changes. In such institutions, not only vocational and job oriented programmes but region-specific programmes are given prime place.

For instance, courses relating to agriculture or some specific manufacturing industry; these are able to attract students in large numbers. What strikes one as very significant is the fact that a band of researchers instinctively follow the leader in making the academic enterprise purposeful. Again, these employees of the open universities do not have any rigid staff roles or administrative or managerial functions. They find joy in doing multiple tasks which ultimately enhance the utility of the course offering. This aspect deserves to be underlined on account of the dearth of trained personnel; it is again crucial in the initial years of the functioning of the open universities.

While much talk goes on about the spread of education in remote regions of the country, not all teachers in India are comfortable with modern technologies, so essential to achieve the goal. The key to solving this problem lies in training and development of the staff, full time as well as part time. An avid desire on the part of open universities to enroll more and more students in a wide variety of courses has inevitably led to a situation of undue pressure on the system. The result is that it is difficult for the administration to spare the staff for training programmes and thus a vicious circle gets created. Ultimately, it all adversely influences the quality and efficiency of the work thereby impinging on the satisfaction of students. This impasse needs to be overcome.

In the Indian scenario, a wing of the Indira Gandhi National Open University (IGNOU), namely Staff Training and Research Institute of Distance Education (STRIDE) has been engaged in exposing the faculty and staff of Open Distance Learning (ODL) to modern practices of transmission of knowledge. In fact, STRIDE originated as the Division of Distance Education in 1985 to meet the training needs of various functionaries of IGNOU. This was upgraded into STRIDE, a training institute for distance education in South Asian region in 1993, thanks to the proposal by COL, Asian Development Bank and the Union Ministry of Human Resource Development. In addition to training the staff of IGNOU and the India's state open universities, STRIDE has been serving the needs of the Asian, African and the Caribbean Countries. Two academic programmes developed by STRIDE must be mentioned here.

1. Post Graduate Diploma in Distance Education, and
2. Master of Arts in Distance Education.

The former of one year duration aims at: *(a)* promoting the concept and utility of distance education in India in particular and the developing world in general, and *(b)* developing the human resources for the existing open universities and DE institutions, and those which may come up in the near future. The latter, one year Master's programme, is designed to develop human resources in various specialised areas of distance education. In addition to these, STRIDE conducts short-term training programmes covering academic, technical/professional, and non-academic staff of IGNOU, state open universities, correspondence course institutes etc.

While the work undertaken by STRIDE is commendable the question arises; how far has it been able to influence the country's state open universities in the matter of training? The number is quite small, only ten till recently with three open universities coming up (Uttarakhand, Chhattisgarh, and Assam) very recently. The three fledgling OUs certainly need a lot of help in getting established as functioning organisations. Whether the other ten state OUs have taken full advantage of the facilities available in STRIDE is open to question. This again brings us to the question raised earlier—whether the state OUs are able to spare the staff for training programmes on account of the pressure of work in their own campuses.

4.1.1. Role of IGNOU

The role of the national open university in India, IGNOU in the development of State OUs in the country is significant and provides much of the context for the development of state OUs. With its considerable resources, both manpower and physical, IGNOU from its vantage position in the capital of the country has been providing a lot of academic support to the State OUs. Indeed, IGNOU may be considered as a role model to the others in the Indian context.

Administering 59 Regional Centres and over 1400 study centres in different parts of the country is not an easy task. And look at the student enrolment—in 2005-2006, it rose to 429,000 and students on rolls (cumulative) comes to 14,33,000. The academic counsellors total upto 48,000 while the teachers/academics are 325 in number. IGNOU is indeed a mega-university. Quite a large number of audio and video lessons were produced in the past few years. The 125 academic programmes (and 1000 courses) cover a wide gamut of disciplines—Computers,

Science and Technology, Engineering, Management, Health Sciences, Agriculture, Social Sciences etc. Thus, IGNOU with its expertise and resources has been in a position to provide guidance to the State OUs. Also, the Distance Education Council (DEC) in IGNOU is extending its help by giving funds to the state OUs. The learners who took IGNOU courses and successfully completed the programmes have benefited both professionally and socially, a study points out. It comes to the conclusion that the students are willing to invest in higher education and are devoted to their studies.

IGNOU has been helping the state OUs in other ways also. For instance, the Staff Training and Research Institute of Distance Education (STRIDE) under the aegis of IGNOU organises training programmes for the staff of state OUs. The Electronic Media Production Centre (EMPC) is a state-of-the-art facility which produces good video and audio programmes in different disciplines and makes them available to the state OUs. The Distance Education Council (DEC) is part of IGNOU's organisational structure and provides research grants to state OUs. It has also taken effective steps for promoting quality research in open and distance learning in India.

4.1.2. Role of Distance Education Council (DEC)

The Distance Education Council (DEC) was established in 1991 under section 16 (7) read with section 5 (2) of IGNOU Act, 1985. The DEC is empowered under Statute 28 of IGNOU Act to be the apex body for the distance education system in India. It is responsible for the promotion, coordination and maintenance of standards of open and distance education system in the country. The Vice Chancellor of IGNOU is the Chairperson of DEC.

Explaining the role of DEC, an official publication points out: "It is the duty of the Distance Education

Council to take all such steps as it may deem fit for the promotion of the open university/distance education systems, their coordinated development, and determination and maintenance of standards in Distance Education in the country." Expanding on this further, the publication says: "The DEC has initiated a number of activities to fulfil its objectives." These include:

(a) Promotion Technical assistance to State Government for establishment of SOUs,

(b) Provision of un-assigned grants to SOUs for staff development, organisation of seminars/conferences, and publication of reports,

(c) Travel grants to faculty of SOUs & DEIs for participation in national and international seminars,

(d) Research grants for promotion of R&D activities in the priority areas of open and distance education,

(e) Maintenance and regular updation of database on open and distance education system in the country.

On the maintenance of standards, several items are listed:

1. Provision of financial support to SOUs and DEIs to promote quality;
2. Training for development of technical and professional competence in the staff;
3. Provision of technical support in the use of information and communication technologies for effective learning, interactivity and development of multimedia courseware;
4. Provision of support to DEIs for transformation of course material into self learning material;
5. Formulation of norms and guidelines for offering professional programmes through distance mode,

6. Maintenance of quality through procedures for:recognition of institutions, assessment of institutions, evaluation of programmes;
7. Restrain institutions from indulging in franchising;
8. Promote high quality systemic research in identified thrust areas in distance education.

The task of coordination is also explicitly spelt out as:

1. Funding for creation of infrastructure including uplink and downlink facilities.
2. Facilitating sharing of Courses and Programmes of good quality between institutions.
3. Facilitating joint development of courses/ programmes between institutions.
4. Providing technical assistance to SOUs for adoption of Credit System and Common Grading Pattern.
5. Developing norms and guidelines for establishment of DEIs and harmonisation of functioning of SOUs/ DEIs with respect to personnel policy, payment of honorarium to resource persons for various activities, etc.
6. Dissemination of information on Open and Distance Learning (ODL) system and institutions to all those interested like government and other bodies, planners and educators, prospective students, etc.

In the Preamble to 'DEC-Guidelines—Establishment of ODL Institutions in India', the following observations are made: "Of late, it has been seen that there is indiscriminate proliferation of ODL Institutions in India. Even single-mode conventional universities are becoming dual mode by offering programmes in the distance mode.... What is disturbing to note is that distance mode has become purely a commercial venture with little or no attention being paid to the quality of education offered to the learners. Many universities awarding sub-standard certificate/diploma/degree programmes are not adhering to even the guidelines issued by the concerned regulatory bodies. In order to safeguard the interest of the students in India and to ensure the quality of education, the DEC has framed Guidelines, 2006, for regulating the establishment and operation of Open and Distance Learning (ODL) Institutions in India". These guidelines cover almost the entire gamut of the ODL scene with clauses dealing with such aspects like institutions that need approval, undertakings to be given by DEIs seeking approval from DEC, minimum requirements for establishment of DEIs, procedure to be followed by DEIs for seeking recognition from DEC and also for continuation of recognition.

Among the institutions that need approval from the Distance Education Council are:

1. State Open Universities,
2. Distance Education Institutions (DEIs) in Conventional universities established by an Act of Parliament or State Legislature/Deemed to be Universities declared by the Central Government under section 3 of the University Grants Commission Act, 1956 and Institutions of national importance declared under Act of Parliament; and
3. Other DEIs registered as societies/trusts and/or privately managed institutions/colleges which are well established and/or affiliated to a university for award of degrees.

While the DEC has its role and function with operational details spelled out in a comprehensive fashion, a spate of criticism from the main beneficiaries, namely state open universities has been particularly strident. This is perhaps due to, as educational experts in India see it, the "big brother" or "overbearing attitude" of the DEC when engaged in the process of collecting vital information so necessary for disbursal of grants and funds. There is no doubt that the state open universities are all autonomous entities, not in any way beholden to IGNOU whose Vice Chancellor is the Chairperson of DEC. As funding and accrediting institution, the current status of DEC is an overseeing body created by the Board of Management of IGNOU whose V.C. is in the same rank as other VCs but who is entrusted with some delicate responsibilities (as Chairperson of DEC) "Exercising even a semblance of authority over one's equal creates, in practice, delicate situations", points out an eminent educationist in whose opinion, a change in the statutory status of DEC is very much required.

Since its inception, the activities of DEC have become enlarged. The DEC has been giving financial support to distance education institutions for a host of activities such as improving the infrastructure, promoting academic quality, staff development and training, and student support services. In addition, the DEC helps the State OUs and other distance education institutes in conventional universities in respect of computerisation and networking. Thus, the DEC is obliged to engage in a multiplicity of tasks. Though these are related to each other, the onerous responsibility of executing them appears to be a daunting task, often provoking some resentment on the part of SOUs.

A large section of the academic community feels that by making the DEC an autonomous entity away from the aegis of IGNOU, a much more harmonious and efficient functioning vis-a-vis the state OUs can be achieved. The way in which the National Assessment and Accreditation Council (NAAC) as an autonomous body within the University Grants Commission (UGC) operates in the Indian higher education system is cited in this connection. The DEC is in fact expected to play a role similar to the UGC in the country's higher education system, the only difference being the State OUs and correspondence or distance education institutes in conventional universities come under its ambit. There has not been any serious criticism of the functioning of NAAC all these years. On the other hand, NAAC has succeeded in creating an awareness of quality and the need for it among universities and colleges in India. The DEC can do a commendable job similar to this if only it is conferred an autonomous status—so goes the argument.

Another pertinent point to be noted here is with reference to the functioning of any organisation which over a period of time gets willy nilly into a track different from what it was originally supposed to do. This aspect comes to the fore in the case of the University Grants Commission (UGC), the apex body in India charged with the responsibility of maintaining and coordinating standards in the field of higher education. True to its name, the UGC became a fund disbursing agency with not much attention being paid to the quality aspect. Luckily, the establishment of NAAC as an autonomous entity under the UGC helped to redeem the situation to a large extent. NAAC has laid down clear guidelines for the assessment and accreditation of universities and colleges in India.

The Distance Education Council (DEC) in IGNOU has also prepared a well thought out set of rules, regulations and guidelines to cover all the institutions in the country operating in the area of Distance Education including State Open Universities and institutes of correspondence education attached to conventional universities. (Distance Education Institutes or DEIs). If, in spite of this, the DEC becomes the butt of harsh criticism, the remedy lies in making it a truly autonomous body whose head enjoys the status of a central university Vice Chancellor as in the case of NAAC. An objective look at the mechanism of

DEC and its way of functioning would suggest the need for a lot of fine tuning in the collection of data regarding all the DE institutions in the country.

There must be a continuous updating of the database relating to the state OUs and other DEIs. This requires urgent attention in the context of the Central Government's thrust towards making Open and Distance Learning (ODL) a vital part in reaching out to large numbers of students. Now only about 20% of students in the higher education sector in the country are learning through the DE mode. The mandate of enlarging it to 40% by the end of the Tenth Plan period (by the close of 2007) is obviously not possible to implement. Yet the fact remains that greater numbers of people are now enrolling in the State OUs and other DEIs.

It all goes to prove that ODL will be the education for the future. And why not? During the Tenth Plan (2002-2007), against an approved outlay of Rs.510 crore the grants received by IGNOU and ODL came to Rs. 248.43 crore. The expenditure amounted to Rs. 232.80 crore out of which the grants to State Open Universities (SOUs) and correspondence course institutes (CCIs) through the DEC totalled Rs. 71.46 crore. But the Eleventh Plan (2007-2012) scheme wise outlay points to DEC and assistance to SOUs and CCIs with Rs.1050 crore out of a total of Rs.8116 crore. This is indeed a quantum jump from the earlier plan figure.

The target for the Eleventh Plan is: ODL should share 40 per cent of higher education enrolment and at the end of the plan, the ODL system should account for an enrolment of around seven million students. Though IGNOU on its own has a network of 59 Regional Centres and currently caters to 1.5 million students, the ambitious target mentioned (7 million students in the ODL system) can be attained only through the DEC extending mammoth assistance to State Open Universities and CCIs.

The DEC plans to accomplish this by putting into operation the following:

1. Content generation with special focus on professional and vocational courses, digitalisation of print material, and resource building for the national pool;
2. Special schemes for open learner resource centre with ICT facility for the benefit of disadvantaged groups and regions;
3. Setting up of ICT cell and centres for certification of skills;
4. Creating Emeritus/Visiting professorship;
5. Research and Teaching Assistanceship;
6. Travel grants/Research.

What about the future of the DEC? Drawing conclusions from the earlier paragraphs, one may reasonably expect a reconfiguration of the council with the badge of autonomy and the head of DEC being conferred with a higher status than now. There can be no doubt that the DEC will be enabled to play a crucial role in the larger context of Open and Distance Learning in the country. The march of technology will help in this process. Again, this will enable socially disadvantaged groups in society to reap the benefits of higher education. This must be viewed against the background of commitments and promises made by diverse political parties in India towards this objective. Social realities can not be ignored for long and the issues of access, equity and relevance are increasingly coming to the centre stage.

4.2. DUAL-MODE CAMPUS-BASED UNIVERSITIES

It is indeed a staggering scenario when one looks at the numbers of students and the variety of course offerings. The 126 dual mode university distance education institutes/centres in India along with the 13 Open Universities and IGNOU are catering to the needs of 5 million students who have taken up nearly 4000 different courses among them. The latter come under a broad list of 430 academic programmes administered through a well distributed network of 110 regional centres and nearly 5000 study centres. Nearly 70,000 academic counsellors/tutors are engaged in the task. There is no doubt that these figures have a significance that can not be lost sight of. In a developing country of over one billion (100 crore) people struggling to create conducive conditions for learning for the vast mass of youth is not an easy job. The fact remains that only a little over six percent of the relevant age group (18-23 years) are now in the higher education stream of ten percent student enrolment.

Whether the State Open Universities (SOUs) in India are able to offer a better quality alternative to the correspondence courses traditionally offered by some campus based Indian universities is a question that bristles with several strands. The traditional campus based universities took some time to start correspondence courses through their own institutes or directorates (ICEs). Thus they transformed themselves from a single mode to a dual mode set-up. Unfortunately, the main objective of these universities at least in the initial years was to generate huge revenues by enrolling large numbers of students in these ICEs.

One may be pardoned for saying that these universities considered the ICEs as a sort of "milchcow" for getting funds. The aspect of quality was not much in evidence, one reason being that the entire experiment was a sort of novelty with no reference for comparison. If one considers the institution growth of DE, one may note that during 1962 to 1975, 22 DE centres came up in as many conventional universities. The growth was somewhat uneven for the next few years—12 during 1976-1982, 4 during 1983-1985, and 8 during 1986-1990. But during the decade that followed 24 cropped up and during 2000-2005, 36 were established bringing the total of ICEs to 106.

These correspondence course institutes in the dual-mode universities were not good examples of efficiency. A spate of complaints from the learners covering a wide gamut of activities continued to haunt the university administrators. The latter somehow smug with the filling in of the coffers tried to cope with the unending stream of grievances as best as they could. In the universities where some dedicated employees were posted to the ICEs, things were found to improve but in the others, it was a sort of merry go round. But students in spite of hardship continued to enroll and universities were happy with the large amounts of money flowing in.

What was done with the huge revenues? Many traditional and conventional universities, instead of using the money for improving the infrastructure of ICEs under their control turned the amounts to meet their own administrative expenses. Very little allocation got earmarked for taking care of the milchocow, the ICEs. In turn, the quality of work turned out by the ICEs suffered. Another negative development was the reluctance of state governments to maintain the block grants, leave alone enhancing them. This in fact was one of the reasons for the traditional universities starting correspondence courses.

Some state OUs in the country have no doubt been able to generate quality courseware and lessons in certain disciplines and this has helped the distance education and correspondence course institutes attached to the traditional universities. The latter have found that they can benefit by using this material with suitable arrangement with the OUs. In fact, IGNOU has provided a lead in this matter by producing high quality printed matter along with audio/video cassettes on several subjects. These are used by some state OUs also, especially the ones without much technical and infrastructure facilities for producing their own material. In this respect, IGNOU has been helping the state OUs in a commendable way.

Looking at the scene more closely, one finds that it is not as if the nuts and bolts for the production of academic programmes are completely lacking in state OUs. It is actually the paucity of competent personnel (academic, technical and otherwise) which hampers the task. Hiring good academics is not easy and it costs a lot in these days of inflation. Almost all the Vice Chancellors of the state OUs who responded to the questionnaire from this COL consultant feel that the faculty strength is inadequate to fulfil the objectives of the OU. Those state OUs which maintain a good equation with the state governments concerned manage to wangle more funds for such components of their work. Again, the question of institutional leadership crops up here.

4.3. LEARNING OUTCOMES

This vital function of any higher education institution, especially the open university, decides ultimately the way in which customer satisfaction is achieved. Here also, the Indian state OUs present a diversified picture with only a few doing really commendable work and the others just carrying on in a pedestrian fashion. There can be no doubt that the faculty and staff deployed for student support services should be people with zeal and a love for working with different groups of learners, the bulk of these being in the category of youth. Frequently, these learners/students approach the student support divisions of the OUs with their problems relating to course material, issue of hall tickets for examinations, doubts about results of tests, and so on. One may say that these problems are mostly routine in nature and capable of getting solved quickly. It is in this sphere, an earnest spirit of helpfulness on the part of personnel becomes crucial. What can be the reasons for dissatisfaction among students? These include procrastination on the part of the staff to even entertain their queries, delayed responses to even urgent issues, rude behaviour and down right rejection.

The Distance Education (DE) institutions cannot afford to neglect these matters. In the conventional or traditional university system, student unions take up several of these issues and force even an unwilling and unresponsive university administration (including Vice Chancellor and his team of officials) to act quickly. In the open university set-up, this type of procedure is not possible simply because the students are drawn from different places and do not gather at one specific time for a class or lecture. Hence a lot of responsibility devolves on the university top brass to see that student satisfaction is not given the goby.

A few general observations may be in order in this context. The section or department for the student support services must be housed in an accessible part of the OU campus and not in an obscure or remote area. Here, the example of a National Open University, IGNOU, may be cited. Here the student support division in IGNOU, is very near the entrance in the campus. The ambience of the place must be such as to encourage the students to ask questions, not stifle them. Brochures and other material based on earlier experience of the students will also be useful in dispelling the doubts and apprehensions of the learners.

Learning outcomes must also be considered as an issue closely allied to student support services. It cannot be denied that the students themselves have a great responsibility for learning and must make full use of the materials given by the institution for self-study in an earnest fashion. This apart, the open university is under immense obligation to see whether the writing of assignments by students is done at the stipulated intervals. Only by estimating or assessing the standard of these completed assignments, the learning outcomes can be gauged to some extent. There can be no doubt that ultimately desirable learning outcomes result when the minds of the students get enriched with more knowledge and a quest for knowing more is developed.

The state OUs in India are still experimenting with different models in this realm without coming to grips with the fundamental issue of crating the mechanism for measuring learning outcomes. The latter cannot be simply equated with results of the candidates appearing for the examinations or the pass percentage in a discipline. However, it must be conceded that this is taken by educationists as one form of measuring learning outcomes. This picture is not encouraging : the university working as a tread-mill producing systematically products as if turned by a lathe in a workshop or factory.

By and large, the state open universities in India have succeeded in reaching out to a very large number of students who, due to various reasons, could not proceed with higher education. This number cuts across different categories as revealed by the enrolment figures. Men and women (gender aspect), locality (urban, rural and tribal), status in society (forward, backward class). Thus the issue of access and equity has been addressed to some extent. Again, the factor of flexibility inbuilt in to the OU system has helped different age-groups to pursue higher studies at their own pace. Indeed, flexibility is the bed rock on which the OU system rests and this has been an attraction to many learners who are already in employment.

Along with this, relevance of the course offerings to the society at large has claimed attention in a few state OUs. The latter have been able to design curriculum details for vocational, job-oriented courses at the certificate or diploma levels with success. Quite a number of takers have benefited by this. Here comes the importance of innovation in the methodology of teaching and training. Not all the state OUs have proved efficient at this task; very few exceptions do exist. This may be due to the reluctance on the part of the OU administration to depart from the beaten track and try out new techniques.

It is rather disconcerting to find a total ignorance of the OU system in many segments of society in India. The state OUs, at least a few of them, are trying to adopt several methods of publicity in print and electronic media with a view to popularise their courses and programmes. Events like the annual convocation addressed by dignitaries get a place in newspapers. Apart from such sporadic occasions, not much exposure to the concept of open and distance learning (ODL) is made available to the general public. This aspect calls for action inasmuch as the disadvantaged societal segments cannot otherwise derive benefits from ODL. Again, this must be viewed against the background of millions of aspirants to higher learning existing in the country without much chance of getting into the formal stream.

Another component to which the Indian State OUs must turn attention relates to a well structured feedback mechanism. At present whatever the OUs gather by way of reactions to their functioning is mostly desultory in nature. This concerns both the current enrolment and also the products who have passed out of the OUs. Perhaps a set-up similar to the alumni associations in some well established institutions may help, though of course, the OUs have only now made a beginning.

Almost all SOUs in India aver that they provide a better quality alternative to the correspondence course institutes in the dual mode campus based universities. It must be noted, however, that a few in the latter category have managed to offer quality programmes to their students. No formal, in-depth study of the products/ graduates from SOUs has been made regarding their employment and job positions. The bias against the SOU and DE mode graduates entertained by many employers seems to be on the wane. This transformation is good for the ODL institutions.

Flexibility available to the learners in the DE mode, especially the SOUs, as regards both subject offerings and pace of studying, has been a great boon to the students. This factor coupled with application of technology (broadcast, audio/video lessons, telecasting through satellite etc.) has also served to draw many students to the SOU system. Here the national open university, IGNOU has been a role model to SOUs. Political support to SOUs has been of varying degrees between state to state. Where this factor was dominant, the SOU concerned could develop fast. This is linked to institutional leadership and where the Vice Chancellor as the executive head of the SOU proved his/her commitment there was no lack of political backing.

ODL has vast potential in India with millions of young aspirants eager to receive higher education and with conventional universities and colleges simply not being in a position to accommodate them. The infrastructure for the expansion of Open Universities is fairly good in the country, especially the mega OU, Indira Gandhi National Open University (IGNOU) willing to help the SOUs. Against such a background, there must be clear indications from the Government of India's Ministry of Human Resource Development about financial and administrative support to the State Open Universities, both already existing and those to be set-up in the coming years.

5

Tele-learning in India

India is the world's second most populous nation and second largest democracy. Nearly 40 per cent of its more than 1 billion people live below the poverty line, nearly 79 per cent live in rural areas, and about 60 per cent belong to disadvantaged groups: the scheduled castes, scheduled tribes, rural poor, urban poor, women in villages and small towns, and disabled. India's literacy rate is 64 per cent, but for females it is just a little over 40 per cent. The National Literacy Mission's drives have been highly successful, but there are still 400 million people who are functionally illiterate. More than 190 million children in the 6- to 14-years age group are enrolled in the 23 million elementary schools, and a further 5.3 million school dropouts attend the 240,000 non-formal education centres. However, there are still 70 million children who miss out on their schooling.

Compounding these social problems are low health standards. The infant mortality rate is 71 per 1,000 live births, the maternal mortality rate is 4 per 1,000 live births, and the protein energy malnutrition rate is 8 per cent. Most of those living in the rural and tribal areas are landless labourers, and in some states, migrant labourers or nomads. Rural development is a high national priority and central and state governments and non-governmental organisations (NGOs) are supporting many schemes that integrate education, training for employment or self-employment, health and family welfare, agriculture and allied activities, and women and child development. These interventions are achieving perceptible improvements in rural circumstances.

It is widely recognised that information and communications technology (ICT) and tele-centres could have a key role in supporting educational and socioeconomic development. However, while the "Scandinavian multipurpose tele-centre" might seem ideally suited to the needs of a developing nation such as India, the country has so far opted mainly for the simpler model of "phone shops." Thousands of these small agencies have been established in rural areas, some equipped with faxes and even computers, all providing services at a price. Even some village clubs now have Internet access. There have also been occasional experiments in tele-conference- or computer-based rural education and training, and some states have strong networks of community volunteers and cooperatives providing voluntary community education and training.

5.1. TELE-LEARNING TECHNOLOGY

Telephone services include basic telephony, leased lines, ISDN (a high-speed communications line), voice mail and data services. Private cellular phone services are available in all metropolitan areas. Telephone connections grew from 4 million in 1990 to 12.6 million in 1996 with an annual growth rate of 12.6 per cent (Department of Telecommunications 1997). The current teledensity (number of main telephone lines per 100 inhabitants) is about 2.7. The aim is to raise this to 7 by 2000 and 15 by 2010. By 2002, it is estimated that 23.7 million telephone lines, 6 million pagers, 4 million cellular phones and 25,000 VSATs (very small aperture terminals) will be added nationally.

The Government of India has recently decided to end the monopoly of the flagship Videsh Sanchar Nigam Limited (VSNL) for international long distance telephony and as an Internet service provider. There also used to be a government monopoly of in-country telephone communications, but now there are private tele-com service providers in three states: Maharashtra, Madhya Pradesh and Andhra Pradesh. In 1998, about 400,000 telephone connections, including 10,000 public telephone connections, were implemented in the state of Andhra Pradesh alone. Across the nation, approximately 44 per cent of the 6 million or so villages have access to telephony and 10 per cent-15 per cent of all telephones are actually in rural areas.

The number of cable TV connections rose from zero in 1990 to an estimated 32 million by June 2000. Privatisation has boosted cable TV which has a potential for interactive service provision in rural areas. There will also be an increase in the use of KU band for educational, health and other government broadcasts. Radio and TV coverage is 97.3 per cent and 87.6 per cent, respectively. There are about 63.2 million TV sets and 180 million transistors in the country and about 43 per cent of all TV sets are in the rural areas.

The Indira Gandhi National Open University (IGNOU), South Asia's largest distance education provider, is now the nodal agency for the sub-continent's first fully fledged educational TV channel, *Gyan Darshan* (Knowledge Network) on the national *Doordarshan* (Television) network, a channel to which it formerly only had limited access. In fact, IGNOU is the only university in the world entrusted with coordinating and operating a national channel devoted exclusively to education.

The computer market has grown substantially, from 1 million in 1995 to today's estimated 10 million and the Internet is significantly influencing the market. Internet access is developing fast, with 50 per cent of users currently connected through VSNL. The VSNL monopoly on international long distance with FLAG (Fibre Link Around Globe) will end in 2000. Private providers, some offering services through VSNL, will have direct Internet service provider access to FLAG, which will substantially increase access to and use of the Internet, including in-country Web hosting.India graduates great talent in ICT—as evidenced by the many successful Indian expatriates in the Silicon Valley. The country has a large pool of software engineers and other technologically trained people.

5.2. EARLY DEVELOPMENTS IN TELE-LEARNING

India launched its first *Aryabhatta* satellite in 1975 and ever since that time has had the capacity to design, build and launch satellites for its own requirements. However, the first application of ICT for education and development—the one-year Satellite Instructional Television Experiment (SITE) which was also launched in 1975 to provide one-way television programmes for 2,330 villages in economically disadvantaged regions—used an American satellite.

SITE aimed to improve primary education, provide teacher training, help improve agricultural, health and hygiene practices, and support family planning and national integration. Community viewing centres were created in villages and the villagers watched these programmes through direct reception system sets. Such communal access was found to be quite acceptable in the village culture. Every resource was fully mobilised to make this experiment a success, but the initial enthusiasm created by SITE was not maintained in subsequent INSAT (Indian National Satellite) projects, which were marred by technical and human problems.

One particularly serious criticism of SITE was that it only provided one-way communication, preventing the queries and doubts of the viewers from being resolved and their responses from being used to improve the programmes.

In 1989, recognising the importance of interaction, the Indian Space Research Organisation (ISRO) determined to conduct some satellite-based one-way video, two-way audio experiments in support of education, mass literacy and human resource development. Running throughout the 1990s, these applications included distance education programmes ranging from engineering to maternal health, rural development programmes covering such topics as the role of women in afforestation, programmes for women and children, programmes supporting *Panchayati Raj* (local community self-government) and industrial training. One of the providers was IGNOU, which in 1995 conducted a 10-day tele-learning/tele-counselling experiment via its OPENET tele-conferencing channel to its networked regional centres and study centres.

Research carried out in regard to these initiatives showed that tele-conferencing could be an effective tool for distance learners, provided it was well planned and implemented. However:

- Interaction was voice-only and, being via STD telephone line, the recurrent costs were prohibitive.
- The quality of audio was inconsistent.
- There were technical breakdowns.
- To avoid feedback, the volume of the TV had to be turned down at the receive sites any time the viewers wished to respond or raise queries.
- Because of the lack of visual cues, learners often had to hold onto the telephone for a long time

before the studio-based resource persons realised they wished to speak.

— The learning centres were not necessarily accessible to many of the potential beneficiaries.

Two parallel developments in using ICT for community development and technology capacity-building are worthy of further discussion: the Jhabua Development Communication Project and the IGNOU Tele-learning Centres and virtual campus initiative. Both of these may be seen as having implications for any use of ITC or tele-centres for education and training, and particularly in the rural sector.

5.3. TRENDS IN EDUCATIONAL BROADCASTING

India's experimentation with the use of mass media for development began early in the 1950s. The Indian broadcaster has, since its inception, been an active partner in educational broadcasting, and both the broadcasting organisations (*Akashvani* or All India Radio; and *Doordarshan* or Indian television) and other governmental agencies have been involved in the production of educational programmes.

Doordarshan's was started as an educational experiment in 1959. The aim was to provide information to viewers with the purpose of influencing attitudes. The first educational broadcasting, done terrestrially, was with higher secondary schools in Delhi with subjects such as Physics, Chemistry, Hindi, Current Affairs, and Geography covered.

Research results from many evaluations during the era of enthusiasm about communication role in the development process left both decision makers and field workers worried. On the one hand, the pace of change remained slow; while on the other, many of the existing perceptions of using media in developmental processes were challenged by contradictory findings from the field. The second major landmark in educational broadcasting was designed to test both the technological capability as well as the social utility of using cutting edge technologies to deliver education.

The Satellite Instructional Television Experiment (SITE) in 1975, as it came to be known, has remained to this day as the major watershed in technology applications in education and development. A quantum leap from zero to satellite communications, SITE was the first and largest experiment in human communication. Lessons from the SITE and other such experiments underscored the critical importance of a multi-pronged approach the application of technology in education. The building up of technological infrastructure had to be backed up by developments on the ground. Specifically, this meant the building up of institutional infrastructures; capacity building; inter institutional collaboration; attention to the educational and development dimension and the importance of social research.

There was no looking back for Indian educators, broadcasters, and technocrats after the SITE experiment. The setting up of massive communication infrastructure began with the launching of India's own satellite INSAT IB in 1982. It is to the credit of the Indian educators that since 1984, educational tele-casts have not only been sustained without a break, but have also grown to the extent that India has its own dedicated channels for educational broadcasting in all sectors.

Teleschool was the project for school children. A Central Institute for Educational Technology (CIET) formed the hub of production activity for school tele-casts with six State Institutes for Educational Technology (SIETs) producing programmes in the regional languages. These were tele-cast on the national and regional networks of Doordarshan.

Countrywide Classroom, for college students on the national public broadcaster was partnered by the University Grants Commission, university based educational media centres and a UGC established autonomous inter-university centre, the Consortium For Educational Communication (CEC) for capsuling and forwarding to Doordarshan for transmission.

The Single Mode Open Universities are also engaged in the production and tele-cast of educational programmes. The Indira Gandhi National Open University (IGNOU) has been broadcasting since the late 1980s, while the B.R. Ambedkar Open University, Hyderabad has been sustaining a radio programme since its inception and a regular tele-cast of educational content since 1999.

Gyan Darshan. The success of educational broadcasting prompted a demand for an exclusive channel for education and the third milestone in educational broadcasting—*Gyan Darshan*—was born on January 26, 2000. Now it is a bouquet of six channels. In essence, it is a cooperative venture with the Indira Gandhi National Open University as a nodal agency for coordinating the activities and up-linking the educational content. The programme mix is a blend of core curriculum based programmes in the areas of primary, secondary, higher, open and distance education, extension, technical and vocational education along with general mosaic programmes in areas of health, hygiene, arts, culture, environment, conservation, science popularisation, etc. In addition, there are state wide initiatives such as the SAPNET in Andhra Pradesh and the University of Goa.

EDUSAT. The fourth major landmark in India's educational broadcasting has been the development and the imminent launch of EDUSAT, a satellite exclusively dedicated to educational and development programming. Proposed under EDUSAT is the deployment of a satellite on the Ku band, and small size, low cost ground hardware. There will be 70 transmission channels available in five spot beams covering the country. The satellite promises high bandwidth two-way interactivity, multimedia multicasting, with a constant rate throughput and adopts an open standard approach for ease of expansion.

In summary, the scenario in the use of satellites in India reflects a system that has:

- An exclusive satellite for education with a capacity of 70 dedicated channels.
- Educational broadcasts on the national public broadcaster.
- Four national and one regional 24 hour dedicated satellite to cable educational television channels.
- A 24 hour TDCC channel available for use in tele-conference support for education.
- A huge volume of educational video content available for all sectors with the various agencies involved in educational broadcasting.
- An unknown but large number of programmes available with Doordarshan, and other government agencies on educational and development themes on a variety of topics and in all Indian languages.

There have been areas of success but there are an equal number of situations that are cause for concern but it is necessary that we briefly identify the key triggers that have enabled the system to survive, sustain itself, and grow. The Indian experience has been with both closed and open user groups and on dedicated and free to air transmission channels of Doordarshan, with a variety of interaction mechanisms from satellite remote terminals to normal telephone lines, fax, and to a lesser extent, e-mail. It has ranged in content from broad general purpose and developmental broadcasting in support of agriculture and basic and non formal education to instructional programme in support of course materials. It has included both simple transmission and interactive tele-conferencing. The experience throws up important indicators for any developing country venturing into educational broadcasting.

Educational broadcasting as it exists in India today happened, driven by the desire to experiment with technology for development and educational purposes and promoted by small groups of committed individuals and institutions.

Emerging out of the broad policy statement of 1952 cited earlier, specific implementation designs, planning, system design, funding, institutional structures, norms and practices came later and have evolved over time when solutions had to be found for problems. Colleagues working in the system have themselves often wondered at the chaos that, at first sight, appears to be its best description, especially as they struggled with making the complex system work. For all its problems and inside stories of struggles by people in the field, many of which cannot be told in public, the Indian educational broadcasting story is a remarkable one; the system has worked and the broadcast of educational content has never stopped, even for one day.

Availability of both the technology and the manpower at little or no additional cost and at a national scale has been one of the most important triggers that have driven the policy to implementation. Today, the Indian Space Research Organisation (ISRO) offers the space segment at little or no cost for educational purposes.

Technology choice has not been determined by access—but by what is the latest available free for use. While availability is itself a great advantage for Indian educators and has been tried and tested, the problems of access remain, and unless these are addressed from the viewer's end, or alternate mechanisms of distribution found, educational broadcasting in India will meet the needs of the very few in the metro cities and will fail to address the needs of those for whom it is intended in the rural hinterland; and will widen, rather than narrow the knowledge divide.

In the early years, there were few or no guidelines, no production capacities or skills in the media centres limited and little or no capacity building. There was little or no quality assurance. Production centres were left to grow as the local host institution or provincial government envisaged. As the system evolved and grew, realisation dawned and policy guidelines, a credo or mission statement, memoranda of understanding and definition of each partner's responsibilities; shared funding, delegation of powers; content and technical quality norms, staff service conditions, etc. were developed. Funding allocation was also streamlined. But by then, it was a question of solving real field problems and of adjustment and compromise between existing and conflicting practices rather than designing policy and ownership patterns as part of system design.

Today, government responsibility remains that of policy definition and the provision of financial resources. Funding and policy is transmitted through independent agencies such as the Central Institute of Educational Technology (CIET) for school education the University Grants Commission and the Consortium for Educational Communication (CEC) for higher education which guide countrywide functioning of their systems respectively.

Production of content is the responsibility of the various media centres established throughout the country in different educational and development institutions. For instance, State Institutes for Educational Technology are responsible for developing producing content for the school sector, agricultural extension institutions are responsible for agricultural content; health institutions produce health content in coordination with the local and regional Doordarshan stations.

Gyan Darshan has been established as a channel owned by Doordarshan; guided by the Ministry of Human Resource Development, and operated as a facility hosted by IGNOU, in cooperation with several ministries and autonomous organisations engaged in the use of educational broadcasting, each of whom funds content development from their own resources and contributes content for tele-cast on the national system.

National and regional advisory and steering committees comprising of stakeholders in the system meet regularly to decide policy and implementation issues. Decisions of these committees are approved by the funding agencies. On the ground, while there seems to be shared vision among all stakeholders engaged in educational broadcasting, and the system appears to be functioning, there are differing perceptions on the ownership of educational broadcasting in India. The consequence of such differing perceptions on ownership is skirmishes and turf fights that adversely affect all aspects of governance and management.

5.4. JHABUA DEVELOPMENT COMMUNICATION PROJECT

Jhabua is a tribal-dominated district of Madhya Pradesh with a population of 1.13 million and population density of 116.68 per square kilometres. Over 90 per cent of the population lives in rural areas. The literacy rate is extremely low at 14.54 per cent. The aim of the Jhabua Development Communication Project (JDCP) has been to gain experience in satellite-based broadcast and interactive networks for education, training and development.

The JDCP Interactive Training Programme (JDCP-ITP) uses one-way video, two-way audio tele-conferencing via narrowcast. The JDCP-ITP system comprises a small makeshift studio and mobile uplink earth station based at the Space Applications Centre in Ahmedabad, direct reception systems installed in 150 villages, 12 satellite-based talk-back terminals, and a transponder on the INSAT satellite. Participation from the receive sites is made possible by VSAT terminals equipped with Demand Assigned Multiple Access (DAMA) (comprising a computer, modem and TV monitor). The anchor person or DAMA operator in Ahmedabad allocates audio channels to particular receive sites as they wish to join in. The DAMA system also allows data broadcasting to the receive sites.

At the start of this project, orientation and awareness-building programmes were organised for the various developmental functionaries and NGOs. Educational and training programmes have since been transmitted five days a week on agriculture, watershed management, health, Panchayati Raj, education, socio-economic and human resource development, and cultural issues. Various presentation formats are used to make the broadcasts lively and interesting and the programmes have been produced in accord with the culture and communication styles of the villagers.

It is now planned for JDCP-ITP to include more villages and to convert the entire system to digital with multimedia, personal computer–based technology and an Internet-based 64 Kbps channel for video.

Formative and summative research has played a central role in this project. The percentage of viewers is typically around 37 per cent-38 per cent of the potential audience, but on occasions can fall to 8 per cent-0 per cent. The viewers tend to be male and the more literate of the population. The frequency of use by high socioeconomic status viewers is low. The main reasons given for people not viewing the TV programmes are lack of time, lack of desire to engage in such activity, and the distances being too great to the receive sites. The village halls used as receive sites were not ideally suited to this purpose. Acoustics and viewing conditions left a lot to be desired and there was often a lot of external noise distracting the trainees. In some cases, the TV sets had been stolen or were not working, and there were occasional failures of computers, audio systems and power supplies. The viewers also experienced difficulty in understanding the "bookish" Hindi language used by the resource persons. However, the conclusions of this study were that, while there might not always be a great deal of actual skills transfer, at least such programmes could promote general awareness among the villagers of Jhabua district.

5.5. IGNOU'S TELE-LEARNING CENTRES

The Indira Gandhi National Open University was established in 1987 and is mandated by the Indian Parliament to promote, offer and maintain standards in distance education nationally. As well as being a major provider, it is also the apex body for quality and standards in India's nine state (open) and 62 dual-mode universities, a role it performs through a Distance Education Council.

IGNOU operates 22 regional centres, 12 recognised regional centres and about 561 study centres that are managed locally by various organisations, institutions, agencies, societies, NGOs and community groups across the country. It has a yearly intake of about 200,000, with about 600,000 students on its rolls, including some students from rural, tribal and disadvantaged urban areas.

The university had gained considerable experience in tele-conferencing, using the Internet and localising educational delivery, and serving learners through community-based centres, even before it introduced its virtual campus through a network of tele-learning centres (TLCs) in 1999. IGNOU offers two programmes through these TLCs: a three-year Bachelor of Information Technology mounted in collaboration with the UK Edexcel Foundation, and the one-year Advanced Diploma in Information Technology, sponsored by the Government of India's Department of Electronics. Students can apply through IGNOU's headquarters in New Delhi or their nearest regional centre and, on admission, they are allocated to their nearest TLC. Almost all of the academic work for these programmes is done online.

Students pay Rs. 67,500 rupees for their three years of study for the Bachelor of Information Technology, of which £95 goes to Edexcel and 40 per cent goes to the TLC. The centres are expected to show a profit from the second year onwards. The course fee covers all course-related expenses including Web access, and the students can make further non-course use of the TLCs' phones, faxes and Internet facilities if they pay for these services.

There are currently 28 TLCs, including eight in Delhi. Until recently, all of them were owned and managed by commercial operators who either operated them exclusively for IGNOU or made the facilities available to other students and the general public in the non-IGNOU hours. Each centre is accommodated in accord with IGNOU-specifications and equipped with at least 50 Pentium computers, printers, scanners, digital camera kits, colour TVs, data projection equipment and antennas for tele-conferencing. The students use the TLCs for live interactive satellite-based tele-lectures or teletutorials, pre-recorded videolectures, laboratory sessions, computer-based tutorials, online chat sessions with peers, faculty and external experts, and Web browsing. They can download their course material via the Internet, but as fallback, these are also available in CD-ROM.

The Bachelor's degree and Advanced Diploma in Information Technology each have a programme co-ordinator, a senior faculty member of IGNOU's School of Computer Science who is responsible for creating the course units and the online chat counselling. Each co-ordinator has the assistance of a lecturer and full-time consultant. Many of the students are happy to work autonomously, but others find it invaluable to communicate with IGNOU staff, fellow students and others.

Students regularly send e-mails to the IGNOU headquarters and there is always one consultant on duty to respond to these. Assignments are submitted online and returned by the same means with tutors' comments and grades. Weekly tele-conferences are held for each programme and locally recruited counsellors provide further theoretical and hands-on sessions at the TLCs. Great care is taken to ensure quality in these two prototype programmes.

A Vice-Chancellor's task force, made up of two Pro Vice-Chancellors—the Director of Computing and the Director of Regional Services—monitors the programmes weekly. Every trimester, academic auditors from Edexcel visit IGNOU for a joint monitoring of all activities including the TLCs' operations.

A joint review committee also meets each semester, once at IGNOU and once at Edexcel in the UK, to review the course content, methodology, staffing and infrastructure. As well, the IGNOU regional centres have a monitoring role, reporting on the TLC's performance to the Vice-Chancellors's task force. At each regional centre, there is also a consultant at the Assistant Regional Director level who is exclusively engaged in this task. On the last Friday of each month, all of the directors of regional centres involved in the Bachelor's degree and Advanced Diploma in Information Technology meet with the Pro Vice-Chancellors at IGNOU to take stock of the programmes and decide upon any corrective measures that may be needed.

The BIT programme has yet to complete its first three-year cycle, so there are no firm research findings on its ultimate outcomes. However, a number of operational difficulties and bureaucratic delays have been experienced. These "virtual campus programmes" operate within the established structure and culture of IGNOU and therefore inherit many of the problems of its everyday operations.

E-mails and other queries from students are supposed to be responded to every day, but in fact there are too few staff at headquarters to handle this—only five of the proposed 35 personnel have been assigned to this task. Constant changes in the consultants also affect the smooth functioning of the programmes. Furthermore, while income is received from students each year, it is not always available for the TLCs when it is needed. As mentioned earlier, the TLCs have been owned by private commercial organisations.

Some of the private TLCs may be retained, but it has now been decided that, with the exception of a few reputable and reliable TLCs, IGNOU and its students will be far better served by bringing these centres under the control of the university and integrated with the IGNOU-owned regional centres rather than being in private hands. So far, 14 of the regional centres have been converted into TLCs and provided with the necessary computer labs for these virtual programmes. The Edexcel agreement is expected to be extended to all 22 regional centres, which will mean that all of the remaining centres will also need to be upgraded over the next year or so.

There are two important lessons in this for any future tele-centres. First, privatising and granting autonomy to tele-centres may make it difficult to ensure the quality control necessary for retaining governmental and other sponsorship and support for educational and training interventions. Second, online teaching and training entails far more than delivering pre-digested content by satellite, Internet, disk or CD-ROM. The levels of interaction and support needed, particularly by first-time learners or trainees, demand considerable staffing and resourcing, both at the providing sites and the receive sites.

5.6. RURAL TELE-LEARNING PROJECTS

The Commonwealth of Learning, with funding from the UK, has initiated an ICT-based literacy project in Bangladesh, India and Zambia. Launched in 1998 and due to end in 2001, this project includes the establishment of technology-based community learning centres to help literacy workers gain in-country experience and expertise and to provide training in reading, numeracy and applications of ICT. IGNOU is a partner in this programme. No evaluative findings were available at the time of writing.

The Madhya Pradesh Bhoj (Open) University in Bhopal, in collaboration with the Rajiv Gandhi Shiksha Mission (RGSM), has equipped 50 kiosks (tele-learning centres) in 45 rural districts in Madhya Pradesh with Internet access and one-way audio/video for rural training via a 64 Kbps dedicated leased line. The plan is to increase the number of sites to 7,000 over the next three years. Here again, evaluative results are awaited.

The Internet has also come to 70 villages of Warana (Kolhapur and Sangli districts of Maharashtra state) where 25 cooperative societies have setup two hubs, one at Warana Engineering College and the other at a sugar cooperative's administration building. This project is supported by a national informatics centre and the state government. Each village has a "facilitation booth" with wireless LAN for high-speed transmission of data for farmers on such essential issues as the best time for harvesting, product prices, accounting procedures, method for processing ration cards and permits, market rivals, new farming techniques, crop varieties and machinery, and pest management. This initiative has enhanced farm productivity, increased the profits of farmers and helped the area's cooperative societies achieve an annual turnover of Rs. 600 million.

In the state of Andhra Pradesh, under the direct supervision of the state chief minister, a databank has been developed on all of the families in the villages in Medak district. Using this, a mobile van provides medicare services to families at a per capita cost of Rs.100 per head per year. The success of this computerised healthcare system has now led the state government to embark on a Rs. 5000 million Sankshya Vahini project, in collaboration with Carnegie Mellon University in the U.S., providing tele-education, tele-medicine, e-governance and a citizen-government interface. This project will be implemented in the near future.

In the Dhar district of the state of Madhya Pradesh, farmers have access to the Internet in the vegetable market for product prices and access to land records. In another instance, in the Ganjam district of Orissa state, the tribal people have Internet access to various information sources, and officials use it for collecting and collating data for further research, with the support of Gram Vikas, an NGO located at Mohuda village.

"Village knowledge centres" have been established by the M.S. Swaminathan Research Foundation in five villages at a radius of 13-21 kilometres from Chennai in the state of Tamil Nadu. Designed to provide agriculture-related information, education and training via ICT, these centres are equipped with PCs with Internet access, printers, CD-ROM and TVs/VCRs. The centres are used to provide the villagers with essential information on such matters as grain prices, women's health and rural welfare schemes, announce grade 10 and 12 exam results, publicise events—even to provide updates on cricket matches! Due consideration is given to socioeconomic contexts, gender and local culture in this work. The centres are provided rent-free by the villagers.

Four of the centres are linked to the hub at Villianur village and all of the centres are powered by solar hybrid systems, the first time these have been used in India. Each village has provided two to four volunteers with grade 10 education to help in the centres and, to date, nine volunteers (mostly female) have been trained in the basics of PCs, MS-Exchange, Word 97, I-LEAP in Tamil and system maintenance. Only 50 per cent – 67 per cent of the females in these villages are literate; 34 per cent of the centres' users in Kizhur village and 50 per cent of those in Embalam are women. About 60 per cent of the usage is voice telephony, signifying significant dependence on voice as the main medium of transaction. M.S. Swaminathan Research Foundation currently funds this project. When the foundation withdraws, as it has announced it will do, the responsibility for sustainability will rest largely with the villagers.

An initiative has been taken by the International Telecommunications Union, UNESCO, the State Government of Gujarat and the lead agency, the Department of Telecommunications of Government of India, to establish multipurpose community-based tele-centres in remote and isolated villages in the state of Gujarat. It is envisaged that these will be used for tele-medicine, tele-trading, tele-administration, tele-learning and other services. A feasibility study and a Memorandum of Understanding were completed and a multipurpose community tele-centre was established in Rajkot, run by a private individual, with land and building provided by the state government. However, this centre could not become sustainable and has now been closed.

5.7. MANAGEMENT OF TELE-LEARNING

The governance and management of tele-learning is based on memoranda of understanding signed by the different participating institutions. Yet, because each participating institutions is itself an autonomous body created either by legislation or statute, governance and management is affected, on a daily basis, by the differing perceptions of ownership. Further, because there are different governance and management practices in each institution, day-to-day system management varies substantially both in style and quality.

By its very nature, public domain tele-learning is a non-commercial activity, and generally does not attract advertising revenues. Funding overshadows all other issues. Cost is the biggest barrier to the use of tele-learning. Funding for tele-learning remains a contentious issue, an overpowering factor determining the success of tele-learning. Partnering institutions absorb invisible costs, while direct costs are provided for funding agencies, and out of an institution's own budget allocations reducing the financial burden on any one institution.

Since the primary purpose of tele-learning is to disseminate particular contents in the form of educational packages, the single most important element in the entire process is the content of the programmes or package of programmes. In conditions such as in India with diverse linguistic, cultural, and geographic realities, content has to reflect regional and even sub regional groups to be effective. The decentralised nature of content production in India enables diversity of content.

India's educational problems are not because of the absence of strategic long or short term planning; but with the translation of planning to implementation. Most developmental projects in India can be accused of this weakness, where the problem is often well defined by policy makers, missions or projects drawn up to address these problems, funds identified, and set aside; and organisations created up to deal with the issue. Implementation gets tied up in knots of administrative politics, bureaucracy, secure government jobs, unionisation and other social issues so that both the goals, targets, time frames for implementation are lost in the process. Yet, despite all the struggles and problems that beset tele-learning in India, one has to applaud the innovative and fresh approaches taken in India to manipulate the latest technological options to address educational needs.

The Indian tele-learning system has both the awe and the envy of many in the world The Indian tele-learning system has benefited from visionary leadership and ground level commitment by institutions and individuals. However, sustainability over a long time also requires that systems re-invent themselves to changing times, needs, and technologies and it is at this critical junction that the system finds itself. Which is why, one has to recognise that there has to be a paradigm shift in tele-learning if India is to retain its cutting edge ability to use the latest technologies on a grand scale to meet its monumental educational needs.

6

Technical and Vocational Education through Distance Mode

In India Vocational Education and Training (VET) is delivered through a variety of government and non-government agencies, at central and state levels. Under the centrally sponsored scheme of vocationalisation of education at the secondary level (1987-88), vocational courses in six major areas were introduced at the plus two level by the Government of India, Ministry of Human Resource Development (MHRD). At present more than 150 competency based vocational curriculum have been developed by the Central Institute of Vocational Education (CIVE) at Bhopal. The CIVE is a constituent of the National Council of Educational Research and Training (NCERT). These vocational courses have been introduced in about 6500 senior secondary schools at the plus two level.

When the Indian economy has been consistently growing at a robust rate over the past few years, coupled with rapid technological advances in the industry, the expected profile of the worker has also been rapidly changing. Further, the demand for knowledge worker is also being increasingly perceived. A survey conducted by the Federation of Indian Chamber of Commerce and Industry (FICCI-2007) reveals shortage of middle level skilled manpower. It is, therefore, felt that there is an urgent need to address this shortage by promoting skill development and for meeting the diverse needs of business and industry in terms of both quality and quantity and meeting requirements of industry.

This leads us to the realisation that there is a continuously increasing number of youth to be trained in marketable skills, so that they can be more employable (wage or self) and can stand on their own feet. The number of dropouts as well as out of school youth who need to be trained is much larger than the capacity of the formal system to cater to in the country. Therefore, the modality of training the youth in the different vocations through the modality of Open and Distance Learning (ODL) is an extremely significant alternative, and needs to be promoted and strengthened.

The increasing interest in globalisation of education might change the direction of national policies, especially within the economically disadvantaged countries, but there is evidence to suggest that ODL practitioners in some of these countries are as attuned to concerns of access and quality as are practitioners in the North. Issues of quality, access and variety are much in evidence among concerns of ODL institutions and practitioners in Asia, where enforcement of standards of quality is embedded in the national policies of some countries and where economies of scale are much more successfully realised than in sub-Saharan Africa and many small states.

Some of the TVET programmes offered are directed and driven more by design for the benefit of targeted groups or communities than for individuals. Planned training provided in this way makes specific impact on the economic welfare of those targeted audiences, whether community groups or special workers. As planned development programmes, they often have their basis in health or agriculture and their impact offer some measure of sustainability where none existed previously. Within the context of TVET programmes for potential learners, however, a much wider range of skills training is not only expected but is also inevitable. This will not preclude more of them continuing to be planned programmes as some of them have been in the past.

6.1. LOCATING TVET PROGRAMMES IN ODL

Considering the impact of TVET cadre of staff anywhere as the lifeblood of service of the nation, their value to their respective nation's economic well-being must be regarded as no less than its mainstay for wealth creation and accumulation. Within this context, potential learners who would benefit from TVET programmes offered through ODL cut across a wide range of educational, social and economic levels. One of the largest target groups, particularly within the developing world, is that of illiterate people. With 72 per cent of all the illiterate people in the world living in nine high-population countries, any planned ODL programmes for potential learners realising a measure of success in those specific countries alone would have a substantial impact on their economies.

Also worth mentioning is that teenagers will comprise the single largest group in the world in the next 20 years. In the developing South, this has already been realised and the level of unemployment among the young is very high. Implementing TVET programmes through ODL will not only transform the economic power of the beneficiaries, the weak economies of the South will improve considerably. Indeed, TVET programmes offer better opportunities for skills training where beneficiaries could become self-employed or established in family enterprises. Given the claim that half of the world's employed labour force is in that category, the longterm implication is that training offered in a variety of locally targeted but employable job possibilities could equip a large proportion of illiterate and unskilled people with employable skills.

TVET programmes offered through ODL need not apply to just those examples mentioned. TVET also responds readily to the introduction of the Internet for more sophisticated ODL approaches to learning, which reflects the other end of the spectrum where course designers develop and modify teaching strategies for a better studentcentred approach with greater beneficial consequences. Thereplication in several African countries of the INADES (L'Institut Africain pour le Developpement Economique et Social) programme in agriculture and that of AMREF (African Medical and Research Foundation) in primary health care is a testimony of their quality and effectiveness. Other potential learners in a wide variety of contexts could witness the transformation to financial security in their future. These include women marginalised through cultural practices, refugees displaced by political instability at home or nationals living in small states where access to educational opportunities are restricted.

All of the above ODL examples have their existence and implementation practices rooted in national or institutional policies. Potential learners could therefore be better provided for where education policies, either at national or regional levels, endeavour to implement TVET programmes using ODL as part of the general education provision. The success of national ODL policies is well established in countries in the South, such as India, Hong Kong, Tanzania, Zimbabwe, Namibia and South Africa. National policies also have the potential of even greater impact where regional groupings are in place, thereby avoiding the potential threat of globalisation. Thus, the implication for potential learners working in an environment of regional economic co-operation to address the requirement for their respective TVET programmes through ODL have far-reaching consequences for successful outcomes.

6.2. DELIVERY OF TVET THROUGH ODL

The effectiveness of the ODL delivery mechanisms has been very well rehearsed. The so-called three generations of ODL practice are still in use, each considered appropriate and effective in their respective contexts. The question, therefore, of utilising an appropriate ODL delivery method for potential learners offering TVET programmes depends largely on other factors, such as the institution hosting the delivery of the programme, resources available and infrastructure requirements.

UNESCO has, on several occasions, initiated moves to mobilise developing countries and spearhead discussions about ODL delivery mechanisms on a co-operative basis. The idea of establishing multi-channel distance learning centres within Africa for use by ODL practitioners in the continent was mooted in 1995—an ideal concept that might have resulted in the development of TVET programmes for all sub-Saharan Africa. In spite of its relevance for this purpose, the pace and widespread use of ICT in ODL practice provides another dimension to the delivery of TVET programmes for potential learners. There are many advantages to the idea of a network situation where programmes could be accessed by potential learners in several countries.

The increasing spread of globalisation of ODL offers the idea of lifelong learning a lifeline across national boundaries, despite economically disadvantaged countries feeling threatened. Furthermore, the potential of launching TVET programmes to a mass audience must have appeal to the volume of beneficiaries. Its merit lies in the immediacy of its impact and the prospect it offers of quality programmes for potential learners whose economic transformation would be widespread with lasting repercussions beyond the individuals themselves.

6.3. IMPACT OF GLOBALISATION

Speaking from an idealistic standpoint, everyone is a potential learner. The move towards the idea of lifelong learning has developed a force of its own that suggests inclusion rather than exclusion. ODL institutions in the prosperous North are expanding their horizons with increasing use of information and communication technology (ICT) as a means of delivery. Potential learners in the North have a lead in the use of the technology that could result in "technology leapfrogging" for potential learners in the South.

Globalisation as a general concept in world trade, finance and now in education is a fluid phenomenon whose impact on the world stage has been described as operating in a Darwinian framework. So, in terms of its appropriateness for the disadvantaged economies of the South, one can speculate about both its worthiness for TVET programmes and how long it will be before it is implemented.

There are a number of factors to consider when attempting to assess the viability of globalisation as a mode of delivery for potential learners of TVET programmes. For example, its impact on the economy of countries in the South has, historically, been negative. This has lead to the vulnerable economies of the developing countries being suspicious from the onset. In fact, the impact on ODL practices arising from World Bank/IMF structural adjustment policies, particularly in the case of recipients of loans in African countries, has adversely affected quality. The evidence of globalisation continues to offer threat to the pessimists, thus making its appropriateness for the delivery of TVET programmes to potential learners a questionable prospect in the immediate future for some countries.

However, another view of globalisation is that it offers positive challenges for the general development of weaker national economies. Potential learners in such environments are seen to have a lot to gain from TVET programmes using the ODL mode.

Consequently, the best solution for those countries is to look for creative economic ideas which combine their well-being, in terms of income-generating schemes, and the political will for good governance. For example, implementation of regional intra-trade policies has been identified as a positive force in minimising the impact of global influence on the national economy. In that context, the view that some countries in the South are "almost integrated into the globalised economy" may serve as a pointer for what is achievable for all countries in the South.

Infrastructure deficiency is usually offered as the main cause of the problem with ODL provision in all sub-regions in the South, even though the factors affecting their respective sub-regional infrastructure may be different. Thus it is possible that differences in economic performance in a South-South context may not always militate against the globalisation of TVET programmes by ODL. Evidence can be adduced in support of this view, particularly in Asia, where seven of the 12 "dynamic developing countries" in the world are located. There, per capita incomes today are at least seven times what they were in 1960. In contrast, sub-Saharan Africa has struggled for years in a declining economic environment caused by persistent political instability.

Per capita incomes there are lower than they were in 1970. Given also that the concept of globalisation is regarded as market driven, its strength for countries in the developing South may be found in joint ventures and co-operative schemes, whether political, educational or commercial, that provide the force to minimise the Darwinian effect mentioned earlier. Global ODL delivery of TVETprogrammes to potential learners has a much stronger prospect of being realised sooner in the Asia sub-region than some may expect.

Further support has been adduced by evidence of buoyant trade results in Asia and Latin America where, for example, economic and political ties have strengthened over a period of time. In turn, co-operation in matters of politics, commerce and education, including ODL, has encouraged the growth of regionalisation against the impact of globalisation. The effect has created a level of commitment which has fostered political stability and nurtured standardisation of good management practice. Such a record of regional co-operation, political stability and vigorous intra-trade practice offers a good prospect of effecting global TVET programmes by ODL to potential learners in those regions.

Looking at the scenario posed by the sub-regions of the South, it is true that some regions are better prepared than others for ODL globalisation of TVET programmes to their potential learners. However, there must be no blanket disregard for its implementation on a sub-regional basis, considering its potential to empower marginalised groups.

6.4. ODL PRACTICES

There is no better way to support proposed ODL practices than to show through examples what has been achieved elsewhere. Limited resources and lives of struggle within developing countries perpetuate underdevelopment, and strategic planning of a radical kind is required to force the pace of change in national and human development. The following examples are meant to serve as a guide to planners of TVET programmes for potential learners by ODL.

6.4.1. Formal Education Provision

There are several instances where ODL techniques have been or are being applied to TVET programmes. A look at the database of the International Centre for Distance Learning (ICDL) will show the range and variety of distance taught courses and programmes available that may provide information about existing programmes for potential learners elsewhere and about institutions which could offer assistance.

6.4.2. Skills Transfer and Collaboration

Regional groupings and inter-governmental organisations like The Commonwealth of Learning (COL) and UNESCO form the caucus of institutional collaborators that offer and facilitate TVET programmes by ODL to potential learners. In Asia, for example, regional meetings leading to working documents, such as the Asia-Pacific Workshop on Vocational Education and Distance Education held in Seoul, Korea, 1996, attest to the level of commitment mentioned earlier. The possibility, therefore, of a mass TVET programme for potential learners is not outside the scope and ability of practitioners in that sub-region. Political will is the key to the solution.

Furthermore, COL facilitates collaboration between institutions that potential learners may benefit from. Just one is the North-South collaboration of distance-taught programmes made available by The Open Polytechnic of New Zealand (TOPNZ) for thetraining of surveyors in Zimbabwe.

However, the most popular training programme in many developing countries is that which uses the ODL mode to provide untrained/unqualified teachers with professional training without having to leave their classroom for full-time training. Botswana, Kenya, Swaziland, Tanzania. Uganda, Zimbabwe, Nigeria, Sierra Leone, Guyana, Bangladesh, St. Lucia and Papua New Guinea have all used ODL courses to train teachers and thereby improve their performance in the classroom.

6.4.3. Non-formal Education Provision

ODL continues to play a revitalising role for developing economies by imparting various functionary skills directly to those whose livelihoods are likely to benefit from the experience. In countries across Africa and in Asia, programmes in primary health care and agriculture have been introduced in response to popular concerns which required the attention of national and local governments.

Within Africa, one notable example is a programme initiated by INADES-Formation, where groups of farmers, the majority of whom are illiterate, agree to study together. The texts, heavily illustrated in colour, visually convey information on what constitutes healthy plants and rich soil. Assignments become a group effort, and the onus is on field workers to ensure that work submitted reflects the entire group and not just the literate leader. Similar programmes also exist in India, but are exclusive to women and are based at the SNDT Women's University in Bombay. This innovative approach to learning offers scope for ODL programmes offering skills training to unemployed youth in the South.

In primary health care, another Africa-based institution of equally strong influence is AMREF (African Medical and Research Foundation). Based in Kenya, its distance education unit offers a variety of primary health care programmes mainly in the eastern and southern Africa sub-region. As in the case with INADES-Formation, face-to-face contact by competent nursing officers provides the interactive support with groups of women to ensure that the essentials of the training are understood and put into effect. Also available is an online programme from Australia for the benefit of nurses working in Asia. Modalities of this kind offer approaches which have been tried and tested for possible consideration in other areas.

Programmes such as these help alleviate the lack of support or access to training, particularly for those living in remote regions. Similarly, in the formal education sector, the ICDL database reflects institutions in the developing countries which offer ODL programmes to satisfy existing, much less potential, demand for their services. In countries such as India, Zimbabwe, Tanzania and Nigeria, degree and diploma programmes in law, librarianship and accountancy are always over subscribed. The reality is that the limited access to these TVET programmes cannot meet the demand made on the institutions but, at least, potential learners living in remote regions are being catered to, which will help reduce the crisis in education.

Development theorists tend to favour implementing programmes and policies which push human and economic activities beyond predictable levels of achievement and immediate comprehension. The possibilities of human endeavour thrive better under conditions offering challenges than in those situations where pace is either stagnant or slow. In the former context, technology "leapfrogging" offers scope to those economic environments where the challenges of globalisation are daunting and where human aspirations are not restricted by rigid parameters. In the latter context, recipients of skills acquired may have achieved limited economic empowerment, but do not appear to be able to alleviate their communities/societies from poverty. However, examples of planned programmes by INADES and AMREF are consequently being replicated throughout Africa, but their impact does not offer enough momentum to transform lives. Besides, the range of skills they provide does not offer a wide participatory level locally in TVET skills transfer.

The Asian sub-region, on the basis of factors discussed earlier, is the hallmark of economic progress and vibrancy that conforms to the challenges of globalisation. It is, therefore, not outrageous to presume that global ODL provision of TVET programmes to potential learners is within the political and economic bounds of the Asian subregion. At the same time, there are countries in the South that could offer similar TVET programmes by ODL using less sophisticated delivery mechanisms by being equally effective for their local conditions. ODL offers enough flexibility that potential learners anywhere can benefit from TVET programmes, whether on a large scale or not. The pre-conditions for technology "leapfrogging" seem to have a basis in economic development and regional co-operation. The African sub-region requires political stability to encourage such requirements to take hold. With that, global ODL provision of TVET programmes to potential learners would have a better prospect of becoming a reality.

6.5. VOCATIONAL COURSES OF NIOS

The National Open School (NOS) established in 1989, renamed as the National Institute of Open Schooling in the year 2002, is an autonomous organisation under the Ministry of Human Resource Development, Government of India. NIOS is responsible for imparting education through open and distance mode from Primary to Senior Secondary level. It has the mandate for offering vocational education and training programmes to general and prioritised groups through a network of its study-cum-training centres known as Accredited Institutes (AIs).

The Vocational Education courses of NIOS are offered at pre-secondary, secondary, senior secondary and post-senior secondary levels. The pre-secondary courses are more of the nature of exposure to the world of work. In addition, the vocational courses are offered as

(i) Package Courses of Certificate and Diploma level which are of 1 or 2 years duration,

(ii) Stand-alone courses are available in combination with other academic courses,

(iii) Life enrichment (non credit) courses and,

(iv) Six months certificate level courses.

6.5.1. Issues of VET

6.5.1.1. Life Long Learning

In the present scenario the learner prefers to do some modules and enter the world of work. When the adult learner wishes to do some more modules, the system provides for that.

6.5.1.2. Credit System and Certification

NIOS has already prepared a number of modules in several vocational areas which provide sufficient flexibility to the learner. When a pre-determined number of modules is completed and required number of credits earned, a certificate/diploma is awarded by NIOS to the candidate. NIOS has a system where credits are allowed for completing vocational course/module. The credits earned by the candidate are recorded and when more modules are completed, the credits are added to his previous score. Certificate/Diploma is awarded when required number of credits has been earned. The transfer credit system provides the learner the much desired flexibility and allows the candidate to enter into or exit from the system as per his/her convenience.

6.5.1.3. Credit for Prior Learning

Recognition of prior learning has an important place in any system of vocational education. Modular courses and the credit accumulation and transfer make it easier to implement it. A learner often comes to a course with some degree of prior competence or background knowledge relevant to the current programme of study. It is important to recognise relevant knowledge or skills of learners and to assign them due number of credits for past experience in the given programme of study.

6.5.1.4. Quality Assurance

The quality of the vocational training programmes needs to be ensured particularly in an open distance learning mode. In order to achieve this, the competencies desired to be acquired through practical work for each module are identified. The Personal Contact Programme (PCP) is then prescribed for a pre-determined number of hours at the work place and testing and certification is meticulously done jointly by the trainer from industry and NIOS.

6.5.1.5. Use of ICTs

The NIOS provides training to the learners through

accredited vocational institutes. These AVIs need to use ICT with the 'human' teacher organising and supplementing it.

6.5.2. Assessment and Evaluation

One of the significant aspects in this regard is to develop the full potential of the learner. The interest, aptitude and capacity of the learner need to be identified before giving the career choice/vocational choice to the candidate. The demand side of the vocation has to be determined by surveys separately. As the population clusters in the hilly state of Uttrakhand are far flung and thinly populated with inhospitable terrain and difficult modes of transport, the programmes for such geographical areas need freedom and flexibility to a large extend.

Table 6.1. Vocational Courses and their Identified Attributes

S. No.	*Name of Course*	*Attributes of Course*		
1.	House Wiring and Repair of Electrical Appliances	A1	B1	C1
2.	Welding Technology	A1	B1	C1
3.	Carpentry	A1	B1	C1
4.	Dress Designing	A2	B2	C2
5.	Computer Applications	A1	B2	C2
6.	Cutting, Tailoring and Dress Design	A2	B2	C1
7.	Electrical Technician	A1	B1	C1
8.	Desk Top Publishing	A2	B2	C2
9.	Security Services	A1	B1	C1
10.	Bee-keeping	A1	B1	C1
11.	Public Health	A1	B1	C1
12.	Food Preservation	A1	B1	C1
13.	Beauty Culture	A2	B2	C2
14.	Plumbing	A1	B1	C1
15.	Motor and Transformer Winding	A1	B1	C1

Fifteen courses suited to the specific needs of Uttrakhand were identified. Facilities for implementating these are also available in the state.The courses have some inherent characteristics and these have been identified and presented through a tripartite, bi-polar classification which is as under:

– Routine (A1)/Innovative (A2)

– Physical (B1)/Intellectual (B2)

– Repetitive (C1)/Creative (C2)

While allocating courses to aspirant candidates, the characteristics of the courses are proposed to be matched with those possessed by the candidates as identified through a specially developed aptitude test.

6.5.2.1. The Test Battery

In view of the criteria of different courses and for identifying the types of students possessing the most suitable aptitude (inherent capacities and potential) for pursuing them, the NIOS took up an elaborate exercise for constructing a battery of four tests.

The General Awareness Test has fifty multiple choice questions with four alternatives to be attempted in the thirty minutes. Of these, 25 per cent of the question are specifically related to awareness about Uttrakhand. Each question carries one mark.

The Verbal Mental Ability Test consists of thirty multiple choice questions to be attempted in forty five minutes. 90 seconds are thus given for solving each of these questions. The Non-verbal Mental Ability Test has thirty multiple choice question with diagrammatic alternatives. In view of the difficulty level the time required for answering the questions of this section, 90 minutes are given. For the sake convenience, it was decided that all the tests of all the sections carried one mark. The Vocational Aptitude Test contains sixty situational statements presented in clusters of three. Each statement has been classified as per the aforesaid tri-partite bi-polar classification possessing three characteristics. The students are required to mark the three statements in each cluster in respect of their liking viz., High liking, Average liking and Low liking. The time given for this test is thirty minutes.

6.5.2.2. Analysis of the Tests

The first three tests are supposed to yield scores as in any other tests. The scores on all the three after being totalled could be used for deciding the rank order of the candidates.

The vocational aptitude test on the other hand has been designed to yield scores in respect of the attributes such as routine/innovative, physical/intellectual, repetitive/creative activity, in regard to the highest or average or low liking categories. These scores could be used for allotting courses out of the available ones from the list of 15 courses at a centre. This is proposed to be done by tallying the characteristics of each of the 15 courses with the scores on different characteristics obtained by the candidate and matching the characteristics. Personal preference and prior experience are also taken into account in this regard.

It may not always be possible to allocate the course desired by the candidate and the one most suitable for him on the basis of the order of priorities determined by the test scores. In most cases, it will be attempted to allocate the vocational course for the characteristics which the candidate has shown preference in the best liked category. The second score on the Average liking areas will be used next and those related to the least-liked characteristics are proposed not to be considered.

6.5.2.3. *The Pilot Try out of the Tests*

The tests was tried out on a pilot basis on candidates from different centres of Uttarakhand in two stages. In the first experiment the tests were administered to a batch of 30 students. On the basis of the feedback, the questions/test were modified. In the second experiment, the coverage of students was 600 in Uttarakhand.

6.6. DISTANCE ENGINEERING EDUCATION

Rapid industrialisation and globalisation has opened up the world, with new possibilities and career options emerging in various fields of engineering and information technology. In India, the impact of such globalisation has resulted in a sudden rise in the demand for high quality engineering education. It is one of the major priorities in the field of education in India now, to make such programmes available to all.

There are two major stumbling blocks towards fulfilling this demand. A brick and mortar solution to the problem is often not practicable due to lack of funds, space, infrastructure and absence of capable teachers. There is a great dearth of sufficient engineering colleges, and even existing institutions suffer from a lack of good teachers and infrastructure. However, rapid improvement in information technology has recently resulted in the availability of a wide range of IT tools, which can be used both for production of high-quality educational material, as well as extensive and effective dissemination of such material to all who seek quality education. This means instructional material produced by good teachers—in the form of video-based lectures, e-learning material, to be accessed by a large number of students irrespective of geographical boundaries. It would thus extendthe outreach of quality education considerably—without phenomenal increase in cost.

Technology mediated learning would therefore seem to be the most obvious solution to this problem.

The other aspect of dealing with this challenge lies in improving the capabilities and qualifications of existing teachers in more than 1,300 engineering colleges across India. Unlike at school level, in engineering education there is no formal training system available to prepare newly appointed teachers for their job. As a result, even face to face teaching varies widely amongst institutions and is often far from satisfactory in many of the institutions. Well-organised training of such teachers would not only improve the quality of education in their respective institutions, but also create a large body of personnel who could contribute effectively towards the production of high quality instructional material, and act as facilitators in future e-learning or blended learning mode.

India has already taken steps to utilise the vast potential of technology to increase educational outreach. The Government has initiated several programmes to promote "technology mediated learning", to overcome the problem of providing quality education in the various engineering colleges in the country.

The "Nationally Co-ordinated Programme in Educational Technology" was the first such attempt to create video-based course materials in different areas of engineering education. The programme concentrated on building up an infrastructure for course production in some of the premier institutes of the country and then on using them to develop these courses. Some of the institutions that participated in the project have produced a considerable number of such courses. IIT Kharagpur is one of the 7 Government-appointed "institutes of excellence" in engineering education in the country. In independent surveys by media agencies, the institution has been rated as the "first" amongst all the 7 IITs in the country for three consecutive years. IIT Kharagpur alone has produced more than 60 full-semester UG/PG courses—which are some of the best regular courses of the institute. These are recorded live in a specially equipped studiocum-classroom through on-line editing. Each course consists of around 40 onehour lectures. The teacher is required to sit at a table and do his "board work" on a blue-tinted paper with thick coloured pens. There is a camera positioned right above this paper that picks up the teacher's "board work". Another camera is placed in the front of the teacher to record the teacher's face when he is speaking/explaining. A third source of input is the PC, which the teacher may use to demonstrate slides/programmes, etc. On-line editing takes place through a switcher which is used to record the relevant camera/PC source at the proper time. Since lectures are recorded in the on-line editing mode, each lecture is ready for copying and dissemination, as soon as the class is over.

The courses are converted to CDs and sold at a nominal (non-profit) price to other institutions. In institutions that have a LAN framework, these courses are often loaded onto an internal server and used in the "video-on-demand (VOD) mode". In both the use of CDs as well as in the VOD mode, control of learning pace remains with the learner, (ie., the learner is able to "stop/start/pause/rewind" any portion of the course). In previous studies using video courses, where the control remains with the learner, learning gain has been found to be very high.

Many engineering colleges do not have adequate faculty in various disciplines. Consequently these courses are often used to alleviate teacher shortages in such institutions and are in great demand amongst both students and teachers as learning material. Use of these course materials in CDs or VOD mode have also been found to be specially beneficial to students having a "language" problem, or other learning disadvantages. Apart from educational institutions, the courses are also procured by R & D organisations and industry as training material for their staff.

The enormous response to the video-based courses produced under the NCP programme triggered the possibility of using video-based instruction to fulfil the extensive demand for training in IT related areas. An innovative off-campus distance education programme was launched by the Centre for Educational Technology at IIT Kharagpur to provide certificate courses in IT-related areas across the entire country. This programme—called the Electronically Networked Life Long Learning (ElNet-3L) programme was not just a response to the rising demands for access to Continuing Education for knowledge updation, but was also an experiment to test several important academic and implementation issues closely related to any large scale Off-campus Distance Education Programme. The aim here was to design a model for a distance education programme that was:

(*a*) Based on the time-tested academic model of "Collaborative Group Learning."

(*b*) Financially self-sustaining.

(*c*) Extendable over a large geographical area while maintaining high academic standards.

6.6.1. The Academic Model

The academic model of the programme is based on a structure where learning takes place through Collaborative Group Learning in specially appointed Study Centres—through "Tutored Video Instruction" (TVI) mode. This is complimented by support material in the form of quiz, tutorials and lecture notes in print format. Six to eight students watch a video lecture for 10 min at a stretch and then break off for a 5 min discussion within the group for clarification of doubtful points. Studies in Stanford have already shown that learning through such "Collaborative Group Learning" methods resulted in greater learning gain for students than when they learnt through regular classroom lectures.

In this mode of instruction, a local tutor would be present, but instead of actively answering questions, he/she encourages the group to clarify their own problems through discussions. Similar models used during satellite broadcast of courses offered by the National Technological University, USA, as well as in a controlled study in IIT Delhi in India has shown high effectiveness of student learning; and in CAI package-based learning.

In the ElNet programme, in instances where doubts could not be resolved by discussion within the group, queries were sent through email to the course faculty and were answered through email too. Over a period of time, the queries and their answers were put in a FAQ file within a group website to help the learners.

Examinations were held under strict surveillance in several examination centres across the country and students awarded a certificate with their "grade" of performance when they were successful in the examinations.

6.6.2. Implementation Model

To ensure proper implementation of the course, financial sustainability and a wide outreach, a three-tier model was adopted, where the academic expertise was provided by IIT Kharagpur, the administrative responsibility lay with a private enterprise called DACP (P) Ltd., and the actual setting-up of the centres was carried out by individual private franchisees. IIT Kharagpur entered into a contract with DACP (P) Ltd, who thereafter looked after the organisational aspect of the course and ensured that the study centres were run according to the norms specified by IIT Kharagpur.

Since setting up of such elaborate Study Centres requires major financial input, to the tune of $35,000 dollars for each centre, DACP (P) Ltd invited individual franchisees to open these centres in different parts of the country, through which the courses were then disseminated. Small groups of students followed the videotaped lectures in the Collaborative Group Learning format. Laboratories were also provided in the centres with necessary hardware and software requirements. The Study Centres had email connections so that the students could contact the faculty at IIT Kharagpur for solution of problems encountered during viewing of the courses.

Within a span of five years, from 1997 to 2002, more than 12,000 students went through these courses in 110 study centres in India and Bangladesh. The programme was immensely successful and feedback collected from students showed a very high level of satisfaction with the programme, as well as with the mode of learning.

6.6.3. Post-Graduate Diplomas in IT and Management

The success of the ElNet programme prompted IIT Kharagpur to start offering postgraduate diplomas in Information Technology and in Management through "mixed mode" in its two extension campuses in Calcutta and Bhubaneswar. As inthe previous model, this mode also consists of Tutored Video Instruction, where courses are developed, recorded, transcribed to CDs and given to students for learning through group viewing and discussion. However, the video lectures are also supplemented by face to face interaction with teachers every weekend. This mode of learning is working well with the added benefit of the face-to-face interactions between students and teachers. However, this face-to-face teaching element itself acts as a deterrent for the model to be extended to cover a wide geographical location. As a distance education programme, therefore, it is not "scalable" and educationally productive.

6.6.4. National Programme on Technology Enhanced Learning (NPTEL)

The aim today, however, is to make "quality engineering education available on demand". It is with this aim in mind that the Ministry of Human Resource & Development (MHRD) has initiated a "National Programme on Technology Enhanced Learning" (NPTEL) which is aimed at developing an organised and well-structured plan for the creation and dissemination of high quality instructional material in different formats of e-learning—including video based, CD ROM-based and web-based courses. These courses will then be disseminated to all engineering colleges in the country—free of cost. It is expected that this would remove the wide disparity in educational standards in different engineering colleges, and help improve the quality of engineering education in the country.

The primary aim of the programme is to use Technology Assisted Learning (TAL) to supplement and not to replace classroom teaching. The design and preparation of course material, therefore, needs to keep in mind the fact that it should facilitate and bring "quality in teaching" to all. The main objectives of the programme are:

(a) Producing video courses, web-enabled courses for UG level engineering education.

(b) Using these instructional material to supplement and enhance classroom teaching across institutions.

(c) Increasing student-staff ratio.

(d) Overcoming faculty shortage.

(e) Using internet multicast/unicast technology for dissemination.

(f) Setting-up a virtual university, in due course.

This programme is a joint initiative of seven premier engineering institutes of the "Indian Institute of Technology" (IITs) and the Indian Institute of Science (IISc). These institutions have been assigned the role of "Partner Institutions" under the programme. In the initial phase, they are responsible for the development of the required instructional material. Other centrally funded institutions like ISM Dhanbad, National Institutes of Technology (NITs), etc. have been accorded the role of "Associate Partner Institutions". They will act as the "user institutions" and in later phases of the project could also act as "content providers".

An initial target has been set for developing 100 digital video-based courses and 115 web-based courses. Both video-based courses and web-based courses have their own advantages. Video courses give an impression of "eye-contact" with the lecturer. They also provide all verbal and non-verbal messages and communication from the teacher and are perceived by students to resemble a live lecture to a certain extent. However, video courses are not interactive. They offer a one-way flow of information from the teacher. To bring in interactivity, it was decided that "administered web-based courses" would be most appropriate. Such courses would be modular in nature and include formative and summative evaluation while offering scope of be administered within an institute by the teachers of that institute. This would allow more interaction between student and teacher through "tutorials" within the institute LAN.

The video courses would be telecast through a dedicated "Technology Channel". Facilities would be provided to all engineering colleges to download these courses for viewing. Web-based courses could be also used as CD-ROM—based courses where there is no internet access. Core science courses offered in the first year of engineering programs, which are mainstream engineering programs, namely undergraduate Degree Programs in Civil, Electrical, Mechanical, Chemical, Electronics & Communication and Computer Science Engineering, have been taken up initially. To ensure that the syllabi of these courses are not too different from those in the user institutions across the country, the common curriculum for all engineering colleges already approved by "All India Council of Technical Education" (AICTE) is being followed. As far as possible, full programs in each discipline have been covered.

The web-enabled courses are being produced in a modular structure, with each module including learner interactivity and formative assessment to help better learning. The aim is to bring in an interactive learning atmosphere in a class. However, at present, a vast number of engineering colleges in India do not have internet facilities. The courses are therefore being designed in such a manner that even though they would be web-enabled, they can also be used as CD ROM-based courses in the absence of internet facilities.

6.6.5. Outreach Programme

Even before the NPTEL programme is completed, there have been consistent demands from the industry for courses in emerging areas which could lead to enhancement of qualifications for the staff. In response to this need, the Government of India has now conceived of a programme called the "Outreach Programme". This programme is concerned with developing courses in video, web and CD Roms for the updating of knowledge on the part of people already working in the industry. The programme seeks to offer a "credit-based education system" where credits can be accumulated to lead to certificates/diplomas or degrees. The focal points of the programme are:

(a) Flexible approach to blend Natural Science, Engineering Science, Information Technology and Management courses.

(b) Credit passbook system which will be updated continuously.

(c) Specific locations of Outreach Education Programme (OEP) centres in the country.

(d) Flexible delivery technology via video and web-based instructions.

(e) Flexible exit option (degree/diploma/certificate).

(f) The programme will be financially self-sufficient.

(g) The programme is now in the planning stage where details are still being worked out.

6.6.7. THE QIP PROGRAMME

Technology provides us with facilities for wide dissemination of instructional material. However, mere dissemination of information does not lead to learning. It is the main role of the teacher to ensure proper design and integration of relevant information into courses for specific groups of learners that result in assimilation and understanding on the part of the student. Only when the student is able to succeed in formative and summative evaluation tests devised according to the specific instructional objectives of the courses, can actual "learning" be deemed to have taken place.In his second role, the teacher would be required to act more as a catalyst in providing inspiration, guidance and learner support to every learner in a course. In the new era, the teacher needs to move from an "instructionist" to a "constructionist" role within the teaching-learning process. He has to become more of a guide, mentor and facilitator. The role of the teacher today therefore is no longer restricted to propagation of information. His role is evolving in these two distinct dimensions.

However, there is a fundamental problem in both the number of teachers available in engineering educational institutions in the country, as well as the lack of training of such teachers—leading to a less effective teaching-learning outcome than would be desirable. One of the steps taken by the Government of India to improve the quality of teachers in engineering institutions has been through the "Quality Improvement Programme" (QIP).

In this programme, some of the major institutions in engineering education—which have facilities for post-graduate education—have been identified as the nodal centres and are entrusted with the responsibility of imparting training to teachers of other engineering colleges. Teachers from Government sponsored engineering colleges are sent to these nodal institutions to gain higher degrees in their respective fields. Study leave is accorded to such teachers to enable them to further their knowledge and research capabilities and gain higher qualifications. They also profit from exposure to effective teaching methodologies through interaction with the teachers in these nodal institutes.

This "improvement in quality" was mainly sought to be achieved through systematic retraining of teachers of the engineering colleges, in the following ways:

(a) A three-year sponsorship for faculty (from the parent institute) to any of the QIP centres for research work leading to a Ph.D. degree.

(*b*) A one and a-half year sponsorship for faculty (from the parent institute) to any of the QIP centres to study for an M.Tech. degree.

(*c*) Organising QIP short-term courses and workshops in different emerging areas for the benefit of the teachers from these institutions.

A study of the usefulness of this programme, however, has brought to light both the positive and negative aspects of the programme. Feedback from teachers who had undergone the programme showed that they often did not consider the programme to be helpful to them in incorporating new teaching methodologies, adopting better evaluation techniques, or providing them with insight for updating of courses in their parent institutions.

Therefore, to be really useful, the programme needs to be modified greatly. One of the problems may have been the fact that the concept of "Quality" had never been clearly defined. A national review of the QIP programme conducted in 1992 states that "Improvement of Quality" includes improvement in the quality of teaching and research, and undertaking of consultancy and projects. The review goes on to state:

> "It is often assumed that since the QIP scholars are all teachers in various engineering colleges, they would be automatically motivated towards improving their teaching/research skills and orientation through the programme.".

It is therefore left to the individual teacher to interpret the implications of "Quality Improvement" and act according to his own understanding. A "Quality Improvement Programme" that includes a clearer focus and training on teaching methodology, evaluation methods, Socratic teaching methods and mentoring would possibly serve the purpose of improving "teacher quality" to a much larger extent. It cannot continue to concentrate upon a means for the teacher to get a higher degree only. It needs to become an enabling factor for teachers and equip them with the means and abilities to help students to learn effectively. It is no longer even sufficient to enable teachers to "teach well". Future programmes have to bring about changes in the mindset of the teacher—to shift their orientation from "teaching" students to enabling students to "learn", to assimilate knowledge, to criticise, question and apply what they have learned.

7

Teacher Training by Distance Education

In many parts of the world, problems of teacher supply, of four kinds, threaten the attainment of the education targets. First, there are shortages of teachers. Teacher shortages continue to dominate the educational landscape. Second, in many but not all countries female teachers are in a minority in primary schools. Third, even where there are enough teachers, too many of them are untrained or undertrained, and the quality of training is often itself inadequate. Fourth, in many countries, there is a national desire not just to raise the quality of the teaching force to match the present demands on them but also to change teachers' jobs as their host societies are changing. In transition countries, society is expecting teachers to change their approach as education itself is being reformed, within the context of social change. And these changes in role and changes in expectation are likely to affect both the initial education of teachers and programmes of continuing professional development.

All of this creates new challenges for teacher education and continuing professional development: the need to find ways of using existing resources differently, of expanding access to learning opportunities at affordable cost, of providing alternative pathways to initial teacher training, of drawing on new constituencies of the population to work as teachers, of using technologies appropriately to enrich teaching and support practice, of stimulating and supporting teachers' active learning and of reconceptualising the traditional organisation of initial teacher education and continuing professional development.

Teacher education has to do a whole range of different jobs: to enable teachers to develop the potential of their pupils; to serve as role models; to help transform education and through it society; to encourage self confidence and creativity. At the same time, many educators often hope that student teachers will develop appropriate, and where necessary changed, attitudes to their job. In order to meet these hopes, teacher education is likely to include four elements: improving the general educational background of the trainee teachers; increasing their knowledge and understanding of the subjects they are to teach; pedagogy and understanding of children and learning; and the development of practical skills and competences.

The balance between these four elements varies in relation to the background education of student teachers, to the level at which they will teach, and to the stage they have reached in their career. Two distinctions are important here. The first is between the initial education and training of teachers and their continuing professional development. The second is between preservice and inservice activities. The two sets of distinctions do not overlap: many teachers begin work without teaching qualifications so that they may get initial training while they are working inservice. Then, inservice programmes may meet a variety of different needs, from initial training to updating or preparing teachers for new roles to helping reform the curriculum.

The needs of primary education have dominated much discussion about teacher education and open and distance learning has been used more to prepare primary than secondary teachers. But this may be changing: earlier expansion of primary education is creating increased demands for secondary teachers, and in some cases to give primary teachers the skills to work at junior-secondary level. Basic education is increasingly seen as including both primary and at least the first cycle of secondary education. Meanwhile teachers who move on to new roles, as head teachers or to work in teachers' colleges, often need and seldom get programmes of professional development to help them in their new job.

Programmes of both initial teacher education and continuing professional development need to match the needs and circumstances of their audience. One size will not fit all. In particular, in designing a programme for teachers, we need to take account of:

- *Their educational background*. This varies enormously between different countries and different levels of education. In some countries there are many teachers with little more than junior secondary education while in others all are graduates with a professional qualification as well. The balance between the different elements in teacher education is likely to affect the content of programmes for them.
- *Gender*. It is difficult to recruit enough women teachers in many countries, enough men teachers in some. Programmes need to fit with the rest of teachers' lives and be sensitive to cultural norms and expectations that affect their jobs. In some countries there are restrictions on women teachers' mobility that affect their ability to attend initial or updating courses.

— *Their experience as teachers.* Again, the content of a programme for–say–unqualified teachers who have just left school may be very different from one for teachers with limited formal education but long experience as untrained teachers.

The teaching force is scattered so that there are logistical problems to be overcome in providing inservice courses. If they have to travel to a central point, then there are actual costs involved for transport and possibly subsistence and opportunity costs for the time they are out of school. Family and other commitments may limit the ability of teachers to attend courses. There is obvious strength in any approach that can reach teachers without leaving their schools for long journeys.

The curriculum of teacher education is varied, and contested, is widely criticised, and in many countries is in a state of flux. In different countries emphasis has recently been placed on the importance of education to help countries compete in global markets, on social transformation, on technology, as well as on developing individual capacity. 'In different places we have got economics, social transformation, personal development, religion, technology, ethics, and a shift in the teacher's role, all among the aims of teacher education'.

As a result, many education authorities are seeking fundamental changes in the curriculum. There is a widespread view that some emphasis, and resources, should shift from initial to continuing teacher education. At the same time, some authorities are beginning to revisit traditional and indigenous educational institutions in order to learn from their strengths and explore the possibility of integrating their work with a more modern curriculum. Demands on teachers continue to grow and become more diverse and their own education needs to reflect this.

Thus teacher education in many countries gives an impression of rethinking, and restructuring of the curriculum. But it is not clear how far the rhetoric of reform has led to superficial or substantial restructuring. The evidence here suggests the former. A recurrent picture is the coexistence of traditional and newer curriculum models within one programme. This takes the form of two competing strands of thinking that, for convenience, can be labelled as traditional and progressive tendencies. The traditional is teacher-centred, based on behaviourist assumptions, has a transmission view of knowledge and regards the teacher as a technician; the progressive strand includes more active and participatory learning methods, is less authoritarian, places more demands on teachers and contains elements of constructivist thinking.

The progressive agenda encourages the development of reflective practice among teachers. As a result, the traditional model of master-apprenticeship, of theory preceding practice, has become increasingly challenged and the coherence between education theory and the actual practice of teaching became an even more critical issue. Key questions then arise for the curriculum planner about the extent to which this agenda is appropriate for teachers who have themselves had only a limited background education.

In a classic analysis of the realities of educational reform, Beeby warned against seeking over-rapid transformation and of the dangers of unrealistic expectations of teachers who were themselves teaching at the limit of their knowledge. All of these issues affect the curriculum planner, regardless of the methods, timing or location of teacher education. If, then, we are planning to use open and distance learning for teachers we need to ask not only about how it can work – the theme of the rest of these guidelines –but also about curriculum policy. Critical questions are about:

- The balance between the four elements of the curriculum for the particular audience, taking account of teachers' own background education;
- The balance between preservice and inservice education;
- The debates between traditional and progressive approaches and views about the appropriateness of defining teacher education in terms of a set of stated competencies;
- realistic expectations that will help the progress of curriculum reform but can be achieved with the support, interest and goodwill of teachers.

The planner then needs to consider methods that will fit both the aims of the curriculum and the circumstances of the learners. This in turn is likely to mean the use of a variety of different approaches.

7.1. TEACHER TRAINING THROUGH DISTANCE EDUCATION

'Distance education' is sometimes taken to mean the use of television and at others the use of the internet. The words imply that students are always remote and never meet each other or their teachers. 'Open learning' suggests that anyone can enrol and start and finish when they like. 'New information technologies' sounds good but vague.

Distance education has been defined as an educational process in which a significant proportion of the teaching is conducted by someone removed in space and/or time from the learner. Open learning, in turn, is an organised educational activity, based on the use of teaching materials, in which constraints on study are minimised in terms either of access, or of time and place, pace, method of study, or any combination of these. Open and distance learning often makes use of several different media. Students may learn through print, broadcasts, the internet and through occasional meetings with tutors and with other students.

Open and distance learning may use print, broadcasts, cassette recordings, computer-based materials, computer interaction, videoconferencing, and face-to-face learning. The essence of it is that it enables students to learn without attending an institution. That has made it attractive for students who, for practical, economic, social and geographical reasons cannot get to college. It also makes it particularly appropriate for audiences that are scattered, and audiences that cannot leave their jobs to attend full-time courses. The world's sixty million teachers are like that.

Open and distance learning is often seen as barely legitimate. Its history is marked by the work of institutions that accepted student fees, gave them poor service, and kept their costs down by encouraging students to drop out once they had paid all their money. Learning at a distance, particularly from printed materials, lends itself to rote learning. If teaching material gives all the answers then there is no room for an individual response while if it fails to do so the student may feel challenged but frustrated.

Distance learning can be a soulless and isolated activity so that dropping out is more attractive than going on. Most parents and probably most educational planners would encourage their own children to study at a conventional university rather than an open university. Few would argue that open and distance learning matches the best of conventional education as sometimes practised in rich universities in industrialised countries or in a golden age we think our grandparents might have been able to remember. But there is a threefold case to be made for its legitimacy.

First, the evidence of public-sector open universities, and dual-mode universities that teach both conventionally and at a distance, is that students can achieve examination results that match those of conventional universities. A significant proportion of students give up along the way and do not complete their courses. But this is true of all students working part-time and not a distinguishing mark of students learning at a distance.

Second, distance education has been powerfully effective in reaching audiences who could not meet their educational needs from conventional institutions. In Colombia, a radio-based school was, in the 1970s, reaching over 100,000 rural peasant students every year. The National Technological University in the United States is using satellite and broadcasting technology to meet the needs of engineers for postgraduate study without their having to leave their jobs and attend a campus. In China, the combined use of television, classroom sessions, and printed materials is providing university education to about a third of all the students in higher education. A church-based nongovernment organisation, the American private sector, and the government authorities in China have all perceived distance education as legitimate because of its power to widen access to education.

Third, where open and distance learning provides opportunities for student interaction with tutors, it allows open-ended dialogue, often regarded as the touchstone of legitimate education. Thus, while open and distance learning may lend itself to rote learning—as does learning in large classrooms—this is not an essential or defining characteristic. The arguments are linked: open and distance learning is legitimate because it has a record of success in terms of the measures applied to conventional education, but would be of little interest if it simply replicated for the same audience what could be done conventionally, and of little value if it got people through their examinations at the expense of more serious educational purposes.

Many programmes of teacher education, in all continents, have succeeded in enrolling students in significant numbers. We need, however, to go on to ask also about completion rates. Where teachers have been promised improved status or pay at the end of the course, completion numbers can be as impressive as enrolment numbers. In its programme to expand the teaching service in the 1970s, for example Tanzania succeeded in recruiting 45,000 potential teachers of whom 38,000 went on to get their qualifications.

In the case studies recently completed by UNESCO, completion rates varied widely. In Burkina Faso, very few headteachers dropped out. In the case of Nigeria, dropout rates varied from 27-39 per cent and the pass rates of those completing the programme varied from 55 per cent to 64 per cent. In the British Open University, completion rates appeared to be relatively high. In contrast, a programme in India had a completion rate of less than 20 per cent while about half the teachers learning about new communications technologies in Chile did not complete the course, partly because of difficulty in paying their fees. In both of these cases, in contrast with the Tanzanian example, students enrolled individually rather than being recruited in a national campaign and were not guaranteed promotion or a new status on completion.

There is evidence, too, that students on courses for teachers get reasonable examination results. A review of nine earlier case studies found that pass rates were between 50 and 90 per cent, figures that are probably in line with more recent data. It concluded that 'while examination success cannot be equated with teaching capacity, we can legitimately assume that a reasonable examination pass rate demonstrates that a programme was effective in teaching academic subjects'. Rather than look at examination results, we might want to examine how well trainee teachers learned. Teacher education projects in Indonesia and Sri Lanka set out to measure learning gains and found reasonable evidence of effectiveness that is in line with the evidence on examination results. It would also be interesting to ask whether the students of trained teachers performed better than those of untrained but unfortunately we have limited evidence, and hardly any of it from open and distance learning.

A series of studies have yielded the disturbing results, from developing-country studies, that there was little difference in school outcomes with qualified or unqualified teachers. One interpretation of this is that poorly qualified teachers are not much more effective than poor unqualified teachers and that there is therefore a case for improving—and spending more on—teacher education. Rich-country evidence bears this out. A recent study from the United States which compared student achievement and teacher policies within its states 'demonstrates that the states leading the nation in student achievement and those that have made the most significant gains in achievement are the states that have the most highly qualified teachers and that have made consistent investments in teachers' professional development'. Better educated teachers probably teach better.

Distance education has been used to reach trainees in geographically challenging areas such as the riverain regions in Guyana, mountainous areas in Nepal, the dispersed communities of the Indonesian archipelago and the small island states in the Caribbean and Pacific. In some high population countries such as China and

Pakistan, distance programmes have played an essential role in providing teacher education on a huge scale. In many Latin America countries distance education has been used widely to support curriculum reform and teacher upgrading. Teacher education by distance is being used to redress inequalities in teaching qualifications in post-colonial Namibia and Zimbabwe and in South Africa, as a tool for reconstruction of the teaching service in Uganda. In other countries, it is being used to reach marginalised communities such as refugees in Sudan, itinerant communities in Mongolia, and minority-groups in northern Pakistan.

Using distance education for teacher training has various potential advantages. Large programmes have brought economies of scale. In contrast to college-based training, distance programmes can provide access to courses on a much larger scale and wider geographical reach. It can overcome regional differences in access to teacher education. It provides a means of side-stepping the slowness and dilution of the cascade approach. In continuing professional development, distance education can help avoid the cost of replacing a teacher who has gone to full-time education. It can open up access to teacher-training opportunities for teachers with family responsibilities who are earning an income and need to remain within their communities.

The establishment of a decentralised distance education structure can also be used to support training in the districts and serve as a basis for the development of a programme for the continuing development of teachers. In print-poor countries, self-study materials can become a permanent resource. It can also 'put information about curricula and teaching approaches directly in to the hands of individual teachers' and cut down the time between learning about new teaching practices and trying them out in the classroom. This is particularly important in curriculum reform and short professional development courses. Carefully balanced mixed-mode teaching can help to double and triple a college's training output per year. Where the infrastructure for them is in place, new information and communication technologies have opened up a range of new opportunities for course- and resource-based learning in teacher education.

Three general points need to be stressed. First, distance education is of potential benefit to teachers because it can reach scattered populations and can offer them education and training without their having to leave their schools. Its has great logistical advantages. This means that it offers the chance of accelerating the supply, or the updating of teachers, beyond what could be done through conventional means.

Second, good programmes of open and distance learning have benefited from its strengths and avoided its weaknesses. Some aspects of teacher education need to be done face-toface, or need close interaction with a tutor or with other students. Others do not. Programmes that combine conventional and distance methods are likely to be better than those that rely on a single approach.

Third, and for that reason, the more successful programmes have been carefully integrated into the structure of teacher education as a whole. They have not been designed as second-class alternatives to conventional education but as a part of a complementary system using a variety of different approaches, each chosen for its appropriateness to the curriculum and the audience.

In many countries there are teachers, or student teachers, with quite limited background education. Often these are the older and more remote teachers for whom open and distance learning may be a more convenient method of study than conventional education. Using open and distance learning to raise the level of their general education may be a simple and effective means of raising the quality of the teaching force.

Extending teachers' knowledge of the subjects they are to teach may be more demanding if it is asking teachers both to acquire new subject knowledge and at the same time to think about how they are to present it in the classroom. In Guyana, for example, a teacher training project dealt with this by running initial, pre-training programmes designed to increases the academic competence of unqualified primary and junior secondary teachers in English, mathematics and science in order to get them to the level needed for entry to a conventional teachers' college Educators have also used distance-education approaches to bring new thinking and teaching practice about specific subjects of the curriculum.

Some aspects of pedagogy or of child development lend themselves well to open and distance learning. Video examples of real-life classroom teaching in a variety of contexts can give teachers a wider range of exemplary approaches than would be possible in conventional face-to-face learning.

Initial teacher education and training is the programme of studies which leads to qualified teacher status according to the official standards of a country. It is the basic or first level of qualification for a teacher. It may be taken as a pre-service programme (before a trainee teacher begins work as a teacher) or an in-service one (while an untrained teacher is working as a teacher). Continuing professional development enables teachers to extend existing knowledge and skills and develop new ones. Some of this takes the form of long structured courses leading to formal qualifications (diplomas or bachelor's or master's degrees). Other forms are shorter, concentrate on skills in managing children's learning or curriculum change and do not lead to additional qualifications. In some countries, qualified and unqualified teachers alike participate in continuing professional development. It may be provided as in-service activities (on-the-job learning) or out-of-school courses of varying length (off-the-job or in vacations).

7.1.1. Role in Professional Development

Initial teacher education is no longer seen as enough. Distance education is therefore also being used to raise the skills, deepen the understanding and extend the knowledge of teachers. Some programmes are broadly focused while others are targeted at specialist groups. Programmes are taken either by individuals or by groups of teachers who are encouraged to participate by their schools or their employers. For example, a non-profit television station is taking the lead on supporting school groups in Brazil. In other cases, programmes are available for individual teachers who want to improve their skills and their status, often enrolling on an individual basis, and at their own expense. Indira Gandhi National Open University in India has a number of programmes of this kind.

In these and other examples planners have chosen to use open and distance learning techniques to meet the needs of their scattered audiences. In doing so they have been able to take practical moves to provide long-term benefits, in terms of their capacity and status, to individual teachers as well as the education systems within which they work.

Distance education has been used for teachers' career development. As they seek promotion, or aim for the next qualification level, or aspire to become a headteacher, or work in a teachers' college, or become an inspector, teachers need to acquire new skills. In Burkina

Faso, over a quarter of the country's headteachers developed new knowledge and skills within four years. This served at least three functions: it furthered their careers, built capacity in the headteacher cohort and provided professional development. This experience, and the demand for specific training and support for head teachers in many other countries, suggests that this as an area of work that merits investment and expansion. It is the kind of programme that will enhance and strengthen the status of teachers.

7.1.2. Curriculum Reform

Distance education can have a role in programmes of curriculum reform which aim to change either the content or the process of education. In South Africa, the Open Learning Systems Educational Trust is using radio to improve the teaching of English, and to support teachers in this work. In Mongolia, radio and print are used across large distances to re-orient teachers to official changes in curriculum and teaching methods within a country in transition. In response to policy initiatives aimed at establishing the use of information and communication technologies in schools, the Universidad de la Frontera in Chile is using the technologies to support teachers who are teaching these subjects.

The Universidad de la Frontera programme, supporting the teachers involved in the Enlaces project which introduced information and communication technologies to schools in Chile, provided an online programme for teachers, as an alternative option to face-to-face programmes and ensured that the course assignments were of an applied nature. Though the cost of the two alternatives (face-to-face and online) were about the same, the online programme appeared to achieve more change, in fostering more familiarity with the technologies and the development of a 'network communication culture' missing from the face-to-face version.

7.2. PLANNING AND MANAGEMENT

Open and distance learning has been applied to the problems of both the initial education of teachers and their continuing professional development, with some evidence of success. The prime task of the planner or manager is to match educational purpose, administrative structure, and teaching methodology. This cannot be done in a vacuum.

The history of distance education is littered with projects that looked good initially but could not be sustained as they were not built into national educational systems. Decisions about such issues as the allocation of government resources, the recognition of qualifications, or the use of teachers college facilities or staff are all likely to have implications for the educational service as a whole. Some of the planning choices within open and distance learning will affect people outside a ministry of education: teachers' associations and unions will be interested in the conditions of service for teachers working in a new role; broadcasting agencies, asked to transmit broadcasting materials, will certainly have a view about the timing of broadcasts and may want a measure of influence or even control over their content.

Identifying the educational purpose is all-important. If the purpose and audience lend themselves to open and distance learning, then it makes sense to explore the nonconventional options open to the manager alongside the conventional approaches of teacher education. The point of these guidelines is not to argue for the application of open and distance learning to every problem in teacher education but to suggest where and how it can be used. The most successful programmes are those where open and distance learning is closely integrated with other approaches to education and professional development.

7.2.1. Policy Framework

The planning of open and distance learning may involve policy issues at international, national and institutional level.

The international issues arise in part because the forces of globalisation are affecting the content and practices of education, in part because new policy issues arise when education is no longer confined within national frontiers. Programme planners are thus increasingly exposed to innovations in teacher education and need to make judgements about the desirability, feasibility and acceptability of these internationalised ideas within their country and programme.

Changes to more practice-based teaching education, for example, have been encouraged internationally and become part of the common discourse about education. This has major implications for the local planning, implementation and management of programmes for teachers. International conventions on the role and status of teachers as agents of change naturally affect national policy. At the same time, educational cooperation across borders, and cross border enrolment, put on to the decision-maker's agenda jurisdictional questions about cross-cultural transference and language and about the control of crossborder enrolment and its accreditation or recognition.

At the national level, lines of responsibility for open and distance learning within government are likely to be complex and do not just lie with the education sector. Increasingly, the development of distance education raises questions that have to be answered within a national communication policy, part of which will be a policy for the educational use of communications. Political, economic, technical and regulatory issues may all need to be considered. Some of these issues concern the respective roles of the private and public sector; educational institutions are likely to seek access to telecommunications on favourable terms, possibly through the use of governments' regulatory powers in the telecommunications sector, or may want more freedom to use telecommunications than has traditionally been available. Other areas to be considered in a communications policy include:

- investment policy, in relation both to the public sector and to the encouragement of particular areas of private-sector investment;
- policy on tariffs and on any common carrier requirements;
- government purchasing policy, and policy for the use of communication technologies for government's internal communication;
- technical standards including frequency allocation, systems reliability;
- the national development of national capacity and expertise;
- scheduling, influence, control over content and intellectual property;
- issues of equity and access.

Within the education sector, decisions about such issues as the allocation of resources, fee policies, the recognition of qualifications, the regulating and monitoring systems needed or the use of teachers college facilities or staff are all likely to have implications for the educational service as a whole. Questions need to be addressed about the most appropriate contribution open and distance learning can make to different levels and types of education, including primary, secondary and tertiary education, and technical and vocational education and training, as well as to teacher education. Questions are also likely to arise about the national or regional location of responsibility for distance education. Many planning decisions will affect people outside a ministry of education: teachers' associations and unions will, for example, be interested in the conditions of service for teachers working in a new role.

For institutions changing to dual-mode status, a key issue will be the balancing of resources allocated to open and distance learning against those of conventional provision and the systematic planning of policies to manage institutional change effectively. This is likely to include new faculty policies (new contractual and workload agreements, training, renegotiation of union contracts, evaluation and support); student policy issues (materials delivery, library access, counselling, financial aid, registration and record-keeping, technical support) and legal policy development (intellectual property including ownership of materials, copyright, and faculty, student and institutional liability).

The use of open and distance learning forces us to distinguish between a number of different educational and administrative jobs that may be done by a single institution, even a single person, in conventional face-to-face education. In open and distance learning functions are divided between different sections of the same organisation, or between different organisation. Where a project or programme is to enrol, advise, teach and examine students it needs structures for a set of different functions. To make distance education work you need structures and facilities for:

— governance, planning, management and funding

— materials development and production
— materials reproduction and distribution
— student recruitment and advice
— student support including the supervision of classroom practice
— assessment and evaluation of learners
— feedback system/formative evaluation
— record systems.

Any organisation needs a governance structure that will make major policy decisions; arrangements of planning, management and funding are likely to be the responsibility partly of people working within a distance-teaching institution and partly of people outside. The development of teaching materials – or their acquisition from outside – is a basic function: distance education depends on such materials. They may be developed in-house, or by external course writers, and are likely to be in a variety of media. An institution will need not only writers but people who can edit materials, so that they work effectively at a distance, and people to brief and train writers and editors. Materials then need to be reproduced, if they are in the form of print or cassettes or cd-roms and distributed.

Broadcasting or videoconferencing also demand a distribution function of a different kind. Structures and systems are needed to recruit students and advise them about the programme. Most students needs support, guidance, and feedback on their work. Where teacher-education programmes include a practical element, concerned with their competence or skills in the classroom, arrangements are also needed to supervise this. Then, in many programmes students need to be assessed and their work examined or evaluated. Finally, a feedback system on the work of the institution or programme as a whole is needed to provide checks on how well it is working while a record system, important for any form of education, is indispensable where students are dispersed, needs to be designed and maintained.

7.2.2. Partnerships

In many cases, it will not be possible for any one institution to carry out all the functions needed for open and distance learning and they will be shared between several partners. An open university, for example, may be contracted by a ministry of education for the development and central management of a programme but this is likely also to involve coordination or cooperation with any national accrediting agency, with curriculum bodies and possibly with public or private-sector broadcasting organisations. Cooperation with local colleges of education may be necessary for the supervision and management of the practical side of teacher education.

Programmes which appear to have been most successful at achieving effective articulation and channels of communication are those that are very systematic in their planning and spend time, ahead of implementation, in identifying needs, on the basis of consultation and among a wide range of stakeholders. This seems to be symptomatic of distance-education programmes and initiatives which have been freed from a pressing imperative of going to scale; which, instead, have recognised the importance of building up a consolidated base as a prerequisite for effective delivery. Key elements seem to include strong programme direction focused on strengthening co-ordination between partners, an internal research and feedback capacity and a concern to pay equal attention to the development of central and decentralised capacity.

In India, for example, a district-based programme for the development of primary education has used open and distance learning alongside other methods of teacher education. It has combined strong decentralised decision-making and management with unequivocal support, if not direction, from the ministry. This support has opened up access to existing state teacher education structures, resources and channels of communication at different national, state and local levels.

In some cases partnerships have gone beyond frontiers. In West Africa, for example, the programme to train head teachers in Burkina Faso was able to draw on resources from educators throughout the region. Teacher education in the Caribbean draws on regional resources through the University of the West Indies, which is owned by the governments of the region. In a recent development, teacher education in Dominica and St Lucia has been supported by a collaborative project with Canadian universities.

Where whole teaching programmes are available across frontiers, these questions about cultural appropriateness are accompanied by issues about accreditation and recognition, and about local and national capacity building. As and when internet courses become more fully developed, educational planners will increasingly need to decide how far to recognise qualifications, obtained outside their jurisdiction, and how far their availability helps or constricts national development.

There are increasingly important regional developments in open and distance learning. The project in Burkina Faso is one example. Within the European Union, the European Commission has encouraged cooperation in all areas of education through open and distance learning and the use of the new technologies. In southern Africa there is a long history of cooperation, including the cooperative development of teaching materials for distance education. From the planner's point of view, regional possibilities may look more fruitful than wider international cooperation, especially if there is a history of educational cooperation within the region.

7.3. USE OF TECHNOLOGIES

Within teacher education, the new technologies have been used for two different purposes. One is training teachers to learn about information and communication technologies and their use in teaching as computers are introduced to schools. In many countries this is being done through face-to-face training programmes, often as part of initial teacher education. Some countries have developed policies which require all initial teacher education programmes to include compulsory courses in the technologies as a strategy for building capacity in relation to them. In other countries, no policy yet exists and teaching teachers about information and communication technologies is at best an option within teacher-education programmes.

The other role of information and communication technologies is as a means of providing teacher education, either as a core or main component of a programme or playing a supplementary role within it. In Costa Rica, for example, the ministry of education developed the use of the Logo computer program within schools as part of a programme of curriculum reform. Teachers colleges are beginning to experiment with the use of computer-based material to strengthen and broaden their curriculum.

In choosing technologies we need to think both about their educational strengths and weaknesses and about the prerequisites for their production, reproduction, distribution and use. If, for example, we want to consider using radio we need to ask who will produce the programmes, how they will be broadcast (by a local or national broadcaster, on what frequency and at what time, and at whose cost), and about their reception, exploring whether learners have access to radio and either mains electricity or an affordable supply of batteries. It is important to ask questions about prerequisites both at the centre and at the periphery: it is not enough to produce good materials if they cannot be distributed or, for lack of access or shortage of particular technical equipment, learners cannot use them. In Burkina Faso, for example, as one of the least developed countries with a scattered population, the infrastructure in place meant that it would be unrealistic to use any medium other than print for teacher education.

In examining costs of each technology, we need to distinguish between total cost and cost per student or cost per successful student. It is possible to justify the relatively high costs of a medium like television where student numbers are high enough to bring down the unit cost. Then, in examining each medium or technology, it is useful to ask three sets of questions. First, we need to distinguish between the cost of setting up or initiating work in a particular medium from its running costs. Next, we need to consider how far the running costs are fixed or vary, usually with the number of students. And, third, it is useful to distinguish between the costs of producing teaching material, the costs of reproduction, of distribution and of reception. At each stage the planner is likely to have another practical question: who pays. For some of the costs may fall on the institution, some on national, regional or local government, and some on the individual student.

The actual costs of a particular technology will depend on local circumstances and it is not possible to set out an international set of standard prices. Even within a single medium or technology costs can vary widely: sophisticated television documentaries have far higher production costs than teaching programmes which consist of a talking head and the equivalent of a blackboard. But comparative costs show a fairly steady pattern.

Costs for the new information technologies are only beginning to become available. Here we need to distinguish between the costs for preparing teaching material and for tutoring students on line. American research has indicated a very wide range of costs for preparing material that is presented by computer, with the lowest where this is simply using the computer to present print and the highest where designers move into simulations or virtual reality.

Where students can contact their tutor by email, they tend to demand more of their tutors' time than when they are submitting a conventional assignment. In the absence of good cost studies of online teaching the only advice for the planner is to welcome the pedagogic advantage of being able to have ready contact with distant students while seeking a way of containing the costs.

7.4. DEVELOPMENT OF PRACTICAL SKILLS

In one sense, all teacher education needs to be oriented towards the ways in which teachers support children's learning and so to the fourth of those functions, of strengthening teachers' practice in the classroom. But there are differences in the emphasis that has been laid on this function between different programmes. Where these are concerned simply to raise teachers' background education, or where they are designed to help experienced teachers learn about new subject-matter, classroom activities may be downplayed.

In asking about practical skills it is therefore legitimate to ask how far this is part of the role of a distance-education programme. The question is critically important for the planner for economic, logistical and educational reasons. The economic ones follow from the fact that the supervision of classroom practice is likely to be labour-intensive and will not show economies of scale. Indeed, if supervisors are to travel and visit teachers in their schools, then the costs of travel may be a significant part of the budget.

From the educational point of view, changed activities within the teacher's own classroom are of the essence of teacher education. This has implications not only for any teaching-practice component within a course but for its structure and content as a whole.

Even theoretical elements of a course, including materials presented in print or on radio, can be designed so that they relate to classroom practice. Open and distance learning has a potential advantage in terms of integrating theory and practice where it enables practising teachers to raise their skills by study at a distance and it is worth seeking strategies that will maximise that advantage.

Conventional as well as distance-education programmes have, with varying success, confronted this need to turn what teachers know and believe into what they do to support children's learning. Many conventional programmes fail to attend to this and some produce teachers who are formally qualified but have had only a token or minimal supervised school experience.

In some countries, practical teaching forms no part of the final assessment of teachers. The issues for a distance-education provider are about managing the supervision and assessment of students in distant locations and how to design materials and activities in ways which integrate knowledge or theory with practice. We can identify five main approaches to the management and supervision of the practicum which are set out in table 7.1.

For some programmes, an overt or tacit decision has been taken against any formal supervision or assessment of the practicum. This has often been the case, for example, where a programme is mainly concerned to raise learners' background education. In other cases, where programmes are aimed at experienced teachers, there is no formal practical element and therefore no need for a structure to supervise or assess it. The Certificate in Guidance by IGNOU, for example, inserts into the theoretical work suggestions about how to extend the ideas presented in the units into classroom practice but this is purely voluntary and not formally assessed.

Table 7.1. Models of organising the practicum in teacher training by distance programmes

Model	*Examples*
1. No practicum offered at all	Certificate in Guidance, IGNOU (India)
2. College-based micro-teaching	Belize Teacher Training College
3. Classroom-based practicum as a separate block in a course, usually placed after academic blocks.	Diploma in Education, IGNOU (India),
4. Classroom-based practicum supervised by visiting staff from college or ministry	Zimbabwe ZINTEC project
5. Classroom-based practicum under the guidance of a mentor within the school	Open University (Britain) Postgraduate Certificate of Education

In the second model, within programmes such as that of the Belize teachers' college referred to above the only practical work consists of college-based microteaching. This cuts down substantially on the organisational headaches of a school-based practicum but severely limits supervision and guidance of trainees' actual teaching.

The third model offers the practicum as a separate block of classroom-based teaching. The Indira Gandhi National Open University offers a Diploma in Education, for example, which has a oneoff block of practical teaching after all the theoretical units. The government of Ghana has explored a model of teacher education in which students spend blocks of time working in a conventional college and blocks studying at a distance while they are working in school. This approach has the benefit of logistical simplicity, and allows cohorts of students to move from one mode of study to another. It does, however, run the risk that theory, done in one block of time, is unrelated to practice, done in another and that the guidance offered by tutors in college is seen as irrelevant by student teachers once they are working in schools. Close integration between the theoretical units and their practical pedagogical application becomes more difficult.

In the fourth model, trainee teachers follow a course while they are teaching and are visited, from time to time, by a supervisor from the college or from some other part of the teaching service. School inspectors, for example, have often been given this role. In principle this should make it possible both to integrate learning at a distance with practical classroom applications. In practice, logistical difficulties have often been overwhelming; in Zimbabwe, where this model was used, evaluation showed that supervision of this kind was the weakest part of the programme so that nearly all the students participating in one evaluation thought that field supervision was inadequate. Where inspectors were deployed to supervise, they had to change their role, sometimes with difficulty. Even college lecturers were reported to 'spend more time checking schemes of work and lessons plans rather than assisting students in the reinforcement of concepts, skills and linking theory with practice'.

In the fifth model, school-based teaching is an integral part of the course, interspersed and often closely integrated with the theoretical units, and is supervised by a school-based monitor. In the case of the British Open University, the university decided to decentralise the supervision of classroom practice to individual schools. This was seen as a necessary strategy to enable students to enrol on the course regardless of where they were living but it also fitted with current national policy of moving towards school-based teacher education. The university undertook the job of briefing and training mentors, who were regular members of the staff of schools throughout the country, and paid them a fee which was a substantial proportion of the total expenditure on the course. The work of mentors themselves was supervised by the staff of the university's education faculty, working from its regional offices.

These five models locate teaching practice in different places. Management difficulties are minimised where it is centralised, as in the Belize example, which also made it possible to use relatively advanced – and expensive – television techniques for microteaching. If teachers are supervised in their own schools, by someone from the distance-teaching institution or one of its partners, it should in principle easier to ensure an integration between theory and practice. While in many instances there have been logistical difficulties in supervising classroom practice in this way either the third or fourth model is one that has most often been seen as appropriate and realistic.

The fifth model, of employing school-based mentors has attracted widespread interest. It depends on the availability of teachers within the system who have themselves sufficient experience and understanding of education to act as mentors, and a structure to brief and train them and to monitor their work. Many ministries of education, in considering this option, have rejected it as unrealistic as these conditions cannot be met. It has also been criticised as a system which serves to replicate the existing culture and values of the schools where the mentors and their trainee teachers are working. On the other hand, in discussing their experience, the Open University argued that their school-based approach meant that it was possible to ensure:

> that all the open and distance course text and resources should be directly related to school practice. No activity, reading or observation could be set that did not directly relate to experience in schools: the link had to be explicit. The course therefore also prescribes a *curriculum of school activities.* This school activities framework is directly related to the course structure and assessment model and allows for increasingly demanding activities, covering all aspects of the teaching role, as the programme progresses.

7.5. ASSESSMENT

There are three separate issues here: how we can make an assessment of open and distance learning as a whole; how we can build in a system of assessment or formative evaluation of quality control within the institution; how we can assess distance education for teachers. In the context of teacher education we look in particular detail at the last of these.

In trying to assess the distance-education experience we are limited by the shortage of good evaluation. One can speculate as to why. Sometimes critical evaluations exist but are difficult to access because they are internal and confidential reports. Sometimes excellent evaluations that are in the public domain are buried within rabbit-warren generalist websites. But the overriding impression here is that distance and teacher education, both together and separately, are under-researched and under-theorised areas and particularly so in developing countries.

If we want to assess teachers' knowledge and understanding, which may be the main aim of a programme that concentrates on improving teachers' general education or their knowledge in one particular area, then there are no particular difficulties in assessing them through conventional tests and at a distance. Assessment can be built into written work relatively easily.

It is, however, still possible to design learning materials, in a variety of media, that ask teachers to undertake activities in the classroom and report on them. This kind of student assignment makes it possible for the tutor both to guide the student and to assess how far knowledge has in fact been applied to practice. The third level, in which we ask how far teachers are in fact applying what they have learned in the classroom, is both the most difficult to manage and, often the most important. Just as managing and supervising classroom practice present particular difficulties for open and distance learning so does its assessment. Again, if this centrally important kind of assessment is to be undertaken, a distance-teaching institution needs to work with partners on the ground, who will themselves need guidance and possibly training in their work. Efforts have been made, using a variety of approaches, to arrange this. The National Teachers' Institute in Nigeria produced a standard grid for assessment of classroom practice by external supervisors. At the British Open University, assessment of teaching practice, throughout the course, was a responsibility of the mentor and school co-ordinator. Students were required to keep a 'professional development portfolio' which included school practice assessments made by the mentor, which was submitted to the university at the end of the course for marking.

8

Digital Library Services for Distance Learning

In order to meet the growing need for educational access and to achieve the goal of democratisation of education, bringing education to the reach of unreached, alternate systems of education have been developed across the globe. Distance or Open Learning (ODL) has evolved as an alternate system making education more accessible to the learner at affordable cost. Today, across the world, the concept of ODL has gained momentum and is recognised as an acceptable medium for imparting education. The revolutionary changes in electronic media contributed to further development of the system and paved way to multimedia instruction using e-materials, radio, audio-visual methods, teleconferencing, computer conferencing and extensive use of internet.

In India, the University of Delhi was the first to introduce distance learning programmes in 1962 through its correspondence courses. Soon it was followed by several other universities. The first Open University was established in 1982 in the country. The Open University and distance education institutions are now in a position to meet the demand for education. India has a vast network of distance education institutions, with around 106 dual mode institutions and 14 single mode Open Universities.

The Distance Education Council (DEC) is responsible for promotion of the Open and Distance Learning (ODL) system and for coordination and maintenance of standards in distance education in the country. In pursuance of these objectives, DEC has taken a number of initiatives for providing support to State Open Universities (SOUs) and other Correspondence Course Institutes (CCIs) of conventional universities. The Council extends technical and financial support for development of infrastructure, institutional reforms, professional development and training, student support services, computerisation and networking for improvement of quality of education. With the recent initiatives of the DEC, about 40 conventional universities have established new Distance Education Institutions (DEIs).

Information and Communication Technologies (ICTs) have brought significant changes in all-round development of the society through transmission of information. Application of information technology to Library and Information Science has provided wider opportunities in archiving and accessing knowledge in the digitised form besides conservation and preservation of the traditional knowledge. Digitisation of materials will provide enhanced access to the electronic information sources and the users can access the digital content irrespective of time and space boundaries. In India, digital library initiatives were undertaken initially with a view to preserve the art, culture and heritage of the country. Some special libraries are also engaged in digital library initiatives in a limited way. However, initiatives in academic libraries particularly in the Open Distance Learning Libraries (ODL) are yet to venture into the digitisation.

8.1. DIGITAL LIBRARY INITIATIVES

Many large libraries throughout the world started

digitising their materials in early 1990s. In 1992 Cornell University formed the digital access coalition to explore the use of digital imagery which is now taken up by the Cornell Institute of digital collection. Launched in 1992, the Yale University Open Book Project has converted its micro filmed volumes of 19th & 20th century books into digital format. The US Digital Library Initiative is funded by the National Science Foundation and was launched in 1994. In UK a series of digital library initiatives were launched during late 1990s. British library was one of the key players in development and digitisation initiatives in U.K. Public libraries in U.K formed a National Grid for Learning and become important provider of Electronic information.

Among the digital library initiatives of Open Universities, the Open University of HongKong (OUHK) Electronic library and U.K. Open University (UKOU) Library are worth mentioning. The Electronic library of OUHK provides access to electronic resources, electronic books and other reference material and can be used at any time, anywhere by its students, staff and faculty. The UKOU also provides access to its learners electronic resources by user name and password. It also provides links to several open access journals and reference materials. International Centre for Distance Learning (ICDL) located in the Open University's Institute of Educational Technology also has digitised library which includes information on distance education institutions, courses and literature pertaining to distance learning. India is also not behind. A number of initiatives are being taken-up, in India towards digitisation.

The concept of digital libraries in India began in the mid-1990s with the spread of information technology, the internet and the support of the Central Government. In 1996, this concept was recognised during the Conference on Digital Libraries organised by the Society of

Information Science at Bangalore. Though a few libraries have made attempts earlier in this direction, the digital library initiative in India is still at budding stage.

Majority of the Digital library initiatives were largely confined to limited uses such as subscribing to e-journals, scanning documents and installing them on the intranet. But there is every need for rapid change in this scenario of libraries in India to use the Information Technology (IT) and ICTs which are confined so far to the prestigious National institutes such as the Indian Institutes of Technology (IIT), Indian Institutes of Management (IIM), Indian Institutes of Science (IIS) Research Institutes under the control of NISSAT and some special Libraries. Some government agencies and institutions, mostly in the public sector are also engaged in digitisation of their libraries in a limited a way. However, it is evident from the initiatives taken so far in this direction that the great potential of ICTs for developing digital libraries has not yet been fully utilised. Some of the important digital library initiatives and programmes initiated across the country are listed in table 8.1.

Table 8.1. Major Digital Library Initiatives, Digitisation Programmes and Institutional Repositories in India

	Institute	*Website Address*
1.	Archives of Indian Labour	http://www.indialabourarchives.org
2.	CSCS Media and Culture Archive	http://www.cscsban.org/html/media_archive.htm
3.	Digital Library of India	http://www.dli.ernet.in
4.	Digital Repository of NCL	http://dspace.ncl.res.in
5.	Digitisation, Electronic Archiving, Indexing and Retrieval system of the Indian Journal of Medical Research	http://www.icmr.nic.in
6.	Digitisation of Manuscripts	http://namami.nic.in
7.	Digitisation of Patents, Designs and Trademarks	http://www.patentoffice.nic.in

8. Down the Memory Lane	http://nlindia.org
9. DSpace @ NITR	http://dspace.nitrkl.ac.in/dspace/
10. ePrints@IIMK	http://etd.ncsi.iisc.ernet.in/
11. Eprints @ IIT Delhi	http://eprint.iitd.ac.in/dspace
12. ETD @ IISc	http://eprints.iisc.ernet.in
13. IGNCA Digital Library	http://ignca.nic.in
14. INDEST	http://paniit.iitd.ac.in/indest
15. IITMK	http://www.iiitmk.ac.in/iiitmk/digitallibrary.htm
16. Indian Institute of Science NCSI	http://vidya-mapak.ncsi.iisc.ernet.in/cgi-bin/library
17. IIT	http://www.library.iitb.ac.in/~mnj/gsdl/cgi-bin/library
18. Librarians Digital Library	http://drtc.isibang.ac.in
19. Mobile e-Library	http://mobilelibrary.cdacnoida.in
20.Muktabodha	http://www.muktabodhalib.org
21. Nalanda Digital Library	http://www.nalanda.nitc.ac.in
22. National Science Digital Library	http://www.niscair.res.in
23. National Tuberculosis Institute	http://ntiindia.kar.nic.in
24. OpenMed@NIC	http://openmed.nic.in
25. Parliament Library	http://164.100.24.208/ls/library/library.htm
26. Vidyanidhi	http://www.vidyanidhi.org.in

8.1.1. Archives of Indian Labour

The Archives of Indian Labour was set up in July, 1998 as a collaborative project of V.V. Giri National Labour Institute and the Association of Indian Labour Historians. The core activities of the archive are Digital Archiving, Research, Collection, Public Interface & Dissemination. It was instituted in order to address the urgent need for preservation of rapidly decaying documents and material on labour and to provide for greater public access to the same, as It was felt that documents and data on Indian Labour are being irretrievably lost due to lack of an organised initiative to preserve these documents in the country. The archive, apart from being a repository of documents also builds collections and initiates research in the field of labour history.

8.1.2. Digital Library of India

Digital Library of India (DLI) is the biggest national level digital library initiative in India. It is a part of the Universal Dig*ital Library Project,* envisaged by Carnegie Mellon University, USA, which has some other international partners such as China and Egypt. DLI is coordinated by Indian Institute of Science, Bangalore and is supported by Ministry of Communications and Information Technology, Government of India. The Mission is to create a portal for the Digital Library of India which will foster creativity and free access to all human knowledge. As a first step in realising this mission, it is proposed to create the Digital Library of one million books, predominantly in Indian languages, available to everyone over the Internet. This portal will also become an aggregator of all the knowledge and digital content created by other digital library initiatives in India.

8.1.3. Digital Library of Art Masterpieces

HP Labs, (Hewlett Packard's) announced a pilot project with the Centre for Development of Advanced Computing (CDAC) to digitise part of the art collection in the National Gallery of Modern Art (NGMA). NGMA plans to put up images of the paintings on the net, from which customers can order full-sized prints. The museum will make reproductions on demand on Hp design Jet printers and sell them. Similarly, the Indira Gandhi National Centre for the Arts (IGNCA) has taken up multimedia projects for the digitisation of traditional artwork and artifacts that will be made available on the web. The digitisation of "Geet Govinda," an important classic of Indian literature, is one of their successful ventures.

8.1.4. Down the Memory Lane

The National Library of India has initiated in late 1990s a digitisation programme, known as 'Down the Memory Lane', to digitise rare books, manuscripts and other resources from its collection. The English books that were published prior to 1900 and Indian books published before 1920 were taken into consideration. Similarly, the Central Secretariat Library has initiated a programme to digitise government publications like, Gazette of India, Commission & Committee Reports, Annual Reports of the Ministries.

8.1.5. Indian National Digital Library in Engineering Science & Technology

The Ministry of Human Resource Development (MHRD) has set-up the Indian National Digital Library in Engineering Sciences and Technology (INDEST) Consortium on the recommendation made by the Expert Group. INDEST Consortium is the most ambitious initiative taken up so far in the country. It welcomes other institutions to join and offers highly discounted rates of subscription and better terms of agreement with the publishers. INDEST Consortium presently include ACM Digital Library, ASCE Journals, ASMe Journals, Capitaline, Euromonitor (GMID), IEL Online, Indian Standards, Nature, ProQuest Science, Sciencedirect, Springerlink and bibliographic databases of Compendex, Inspec and MathSciNet.

8.1.6. Kalasampada

Indira Gandhi National Centre for Arts (IGNCA),

established a Digital Library, known as "Kalasampada", (Digital Library Resource for Indian Cultural Heritage). It includes non-print as well as printed materials. The users will have access to the highly researched publications of the IGNCA from a single window. The integration of multimedia computer technology and software provides a new dimension in the study of the Indian Art and Culture.

8.1.7. Khuda Baksh Oriental Public Library

The Khuda Baksh Oriential Public Library has initiated digitisation of Arabic and Persian manuscripts of the medieval India. It is one of the Oriental Libraries having rich collection of Persian, Arabic, Urdu and other languages manuscripts.

8.1.8. Mobile Digital Library

For spreading and promoting literacy among the common citizens, Internet enabled Mobile Digital Library was brought to use. Mobile Van with satellite connection for Internet connectivity is used. The van is also fitted with printer, and binding machine for providing bound books to the end user from a single point. This is a product from C-DAC-ERDC Noida.

8.1.9. Mukhtabodha Digital Library and Archiving Project

The Mukhtabodha Project is an attempt to create a digital library in Indian languages specially the ancient texts on palm leaves, birch tree barks etc.

8.1.10. National Institute of Advanced Studies (NIAS), Bangalore

This institution has started digitisation of paintings and the Microfilming of Indian Publication Project (MIPP).

The NIAS has also started work on rare manuscript preservation projects for both microfilm and microfiche.

8.1.11. National Mission for Manuscripts

The Department of Culture, Government of India has launched the 'National Mission for Manuscripts' in 2003 with the main objectives of conservation and preservation of Manuscripts for posterity. India, being the largest repository of Manuscripts, rare books, classics etc., urgently needs digitisation to preserve as well as give access to. The National Informatics Centre (NIC) has prepared detailed guidelines for digitisation of Manuscripts.

8.1.12. National Resource Centre for Women

The National Resource Centre for Women was set-up by the Government of India as a Virtual Resource Centre on Women's issues. It serves as a decentralised, participatory and partnership oriented entity aiming at giving access to digital catalogues of different libraries dealing with women's issues, reports of diverse nature, statistics, events, legislation etc using different media to reach the clientele at different levels.

8.1.13. Parliament Library

In order to cater to the needs of Members of Parliament and officers and staff of Parliament Secretariat a digital library has been set-up in the parliament library. A large number of index-based databases of information was initially developed by the computer centre. The data stored and available now in PARLIS databases for online retrieval relates to questions, debates, reports, bio-data of present and past members of parliament including photographs and addresses etc.

8.1.14. Vidyanidhi

Vidyanidhi–a Sanskrit word means "Treasure of Knowledge". It is begun as a pilot project to demonstrate the feasibility of electronic Theses and Dissertations. As per the Action Plan of the National Task Force on Information Technology and Software Development, it is mandatory for all universities and deemed universities across the country to host every thesis/ dissertation on a designated website. This national policy has provided a policy framework for initiating a digital library of ETDs. 'Vidyanidhi' project was started in the year 2000 at the Department of Library and Information Science, University of Mysore, with the sponsorship of National Information System for Science and Technology, Government of India. The Project's vision is to build and strengthen the research capacities and enhance the quality of doctoral research in India.

8.2. PROBLEMS OF DIGITAL LIBRARIES

The digitisation initiatives in India are encountered with the problems of lack of technical infrastructure, trained manpower, finances and policy initiatives. Some of the problems are:

- Lack of clear cut policy at National level with main focus on sustainability.
- Outdated software and hardware and difficulty in upgrading the same.
- Non-availability of cost effective new technological advancement.
- Lack of multiple Indian language OCR facilities.
- Non-standard technical activities, data description and transmission characteristics.
- Non-availability of well-trained skilled personnel.

- Lack of management support.
- Lack of proper preservation policy.
- No Intellectual Property Rights policy for content development of digital information.
- Rigidity in the publishers' policies and data formats.

The above factors affect the success of digitisation initiatives and the creation of digital libraries. These problems have to be addressed positively to ensure planned digital resource development programmes and digital libraries in the country. In order to achieve it, the following factors may be taken into consideration.

National Policy for Digitisation: Should focus on:

- Education and life long learning for all citizens.
- Information to enhance participation of citizens in the socio-economic development.
- Promotion of business and economy, training and employment.
- Traditional knowledge and preservation of cultural heritage.
- Developing repository of historical evidence and community history.

8.2.1. Sustainability Issues

For issues related to sustainability, the main focus will have to be on the following areas:

- User focused policy and strategies.
- Provision for refreshing the data.
- User charges, prices, framing guidelines for fixation of prices.
- People's participation, Political and administrative will.

- Capacity building to develop skilled man power.
- Co-operative subscriptions, shared technology system, resource sharing, joint archives.
- Changing role of librarians and information professionals.

8.2.2. Digital Divide

The major issues to be addressed in India before taking initiatives to create the digital libraries are:

- Creation of basic infrastructural facilities such as internet and telecommunications etc.
- Creation of awareness among the users on usage of technology.

8.3. STUDENTS' NEEDS

Distance students' characteristics are different from students in traditional universities. They are generally adult learners, mature, employed, and have family responsibilities. They have higher motivation and are willing to take responsibility for their own education. Their goals are often more clear cut. Distance students are self-directed, study on independent basis. They learn in a variety of ways and take control over their learning. They often experience a feeling of isolation and remoteness from other students. Distance learners access to library and educational resources and services in various ways. Access can be directed e.g. face to face, or mediated by printed material, e.g. manuals, brochure, or mediated by technology, using a variety of media such as telephone, voice mail, web site, email. Successful direct access is characterised by flexibility, reliability, availability, user-friendly, portability, efficiency and service ability.

Library services are essential support services to distance education students. Most researchers in distance learning are in agreement that library support is a key element. Distance learners expectations of library services as revealed in the literature, demonstrate a great need . The library needs of distant learners arc not unique; they have the same library and information needs as on campus students. Apart from the manner in which they are accessed, requested and delivered, the same resources are required, the same questions are asked, and the same quality of service is expected; and they expect the same level of library service as that provided to their peers on campus. Effective and appropriate services to distance learning communities may differ from, but must be equivalent to those services offered on a traditional campus. They frequently find the following problems in using library resources and services.

- Their institution may not offer a library service; they may face delays and expense in contacting the library or there are many barriers that students give up trying to use it.
- Their library expectations are often low.
- They lack information literacy skill, they frequently do not know or do not find out what services and resources are available or how to access them.
- They frequently possess inadequately knowledge and experience in library research, electronic informational resources, and technology in general.
- They may never come on campus so that they rarely receive information literacy training and are unable to use in-person assistance from librarians.

8.4. IMPORTANCE OF INFORMATION LITERACY

Information literacy which was developed from library instruction has been the term most frequently used since the late nineteenth. Information literacy is considered a survival skill for the new century, the key competency for independent study, self-directed learner, lifelong learning, and the foundation of a literate society. Information literacy is important to student achievement and considered a desirable outcome of higher education. Information literacy competencies are desirable for all graduates. Through information literacy, the other literacies can be achieved. Many studies, research reports and articles theorising and describing the importance and needs of information literacy skills and instructions. However less research has been done on information literacy instruction to distance students.

Information literacy becomes more important in the escalating complexed environment:

- *The information environment*: E.g. the information explosion, unimaginable expansion information, proliferating information resource, unfiltered formats and multiple media of information, diverse, abundant information choices – in the academic students, in the workplace and in the personnel lives of individuals.
- *The technological environment*: E.g. rapid technological change; increase dependence technology for daily tasks.
- *The educational reform environment*: E.g. pedagogical methodologies transform by the focus on educational reform; some new pedagogical strategies including resource- based teaching/ learning; project -based teaching/learning; research-based teaching/learning; outcomes-basedteaching/ learning

The many changes in the society especially in higher education and distance education environment present numerous responsibilities to academic librarians and have given them opportunities to take more central roles in the distance education process. The educational roles of academic librarians are expanding especially in teaching library/ information skills. The ACRL (Association of College and Research Libraries) Guidelines for Distancc Learning Library Services delineated the elements necessary for institutions of higher education to support the distance learning programme and to meet the needs of the faculty, students and academic support staff. The Guidelines assumes many important precepts which shape the roles of librarians and the management of distance learning library services.

The instilling of lifelong learning skills through general bibliographic and information literacy instruction in academic libraries is a primary outcome of higher education Such preparation and measurement of its outcomes are of equal necessity for the distance learning community as for those on the traditional campus.

Librarians' roles in teaching information literacy skills among distance students and independent learning programme have produced a considerable amount of literature. Involvement in building information literacy skills is one important role even in the online environment. Librarians can contribute actively by providing distance learners with various forms of information literacy instruction for effective use of library and information resources and services and ensure that students are made aware of their critical role and importance to their learning. Some formats of information literacy instruction include face to face, workshops, credit course, booklets, printed materials, videotapes, cassette tapes, CD ROM s, online courses, web-based courses, and other innovative methods using technology.

The ACRL Guidelines for Instruction Programmes in Academic Libraries identified various modes of instruction:

> These may include, but are not limited to: advising individuals at reference desks, in-depth research consultations, individualised instruction-electronic or print instruction aids, or group instruction traditional or electronic classroom settings. The mode(s) selected should be consistent with the content and goals of instruction. Where appropriate, more than one mode of instruction should be used in recognition of the wide variety of learning styles of individuals.

Faculty members and librarians share roles in helping students acquire information literacy skills effectively and become information literate. The ALA Presidential Committee on Information Literacy stated that to be information literate, a person must be able to recognise when information is needed and have the ability to locate, evaluate and use effectively the needed information.

Librarians have been seen as partners with faculty members in integrating information literacy in higher education curriculum. The development of information literacy is purported to be especially successful when librarians develop partnerships with faculty members and as partners, incorporate information literacy programmes into the academic curriculum. Emerging critical roles for librarians include working with academics to ensure appropriate inclusion of information seeking in courses offered in flexible delivery mode; seeking out membership in course development teams.

8.5. DIGITAL LIBRARY'S CONTRIBUTIONS TO DISTANCE LEARNERS

Distance Learners' characteristics are different from

students in the traditional universities. They are generally adults, employed and have family responsibilities. Their motivation levels are generally high and are willing to take responsibility for their own education. Mostly they are self-directed and study on independent basis. They choose a variety of ways for learning and take control over their learning. They are mainly constrained by the problems of access and retrieval of the required information from libraries. The problems are:

- The distance learning institution may not offer library services to the learners.
- Learners have reluctance to travel long distances to use the library.
- Lack of information literacy skills.
- Lack of knowledge in using libraries or using electronic information sources.
- Reluctance to approach the librarian and library staff members for help in retrieving the information.

Digital library provides an answer to most of the information access problems of the distance learners. Today, ODL institutions bring education at the doorsteps of the learners through networks. The Internet also plays a vital role in acting as a powerful tool to the learners. Digitisation of scholarly materials is one of the many initiatives undertaken by institutions across the globe, which facilitates wide access and availability of such materials.

The ODL institutions can initiate a consortium that will plan, co-ordinate and implement a national level digital library for the benefit of distance learners. Each individual member institution of the consortium should share its learning resources. This way, a wide range of collection of learning materials can be developed. This should be made available to the learners and accessible through the Intranet and the Internet. A digital rights management system can be interlinked with the digital library to address the copyrights and other related issues. Copy right laws are very old in India and need to be amended keeping in view of the digitisation. In the proposed consortium approach all the participating open universities should come to a consensus on the copy right issues to promote open access initiative.

India has one Open University at the national level and 13 State Open Universities offering courses only in distance mode. These universities have libraries to meet the information needs of their learners. All these universities subscribe to several high value journals with substantial duplication. In addition, they publish newsletters, annual reports, thesis, course materials, old question papers etc., which are important resources for the learners.

The duplication of resources can be avoided, if a nodal agency is formed under the aegis of Distance Education Council. This nodal agency will create necessary infrastructure to network the digitised resources of all the universities and rationalise the access of the high valued electronic journals and other resources.

There are several digital libraries for distance learning in the world which are highly successful (ICDL, Hong Kong Open University etc). Similarly In India also an attempt has been made in this direction by establishing INDEST and Infonet consortia.

All the open universities should come to an understanding regarding digitisation of the material and networking of the resources for implementation in a phased manner.

The nodal agency will provide access to all the member ODL institutions:

- Online databases.
- Online electronic journals in various subject disciplines.
- 'Research in progress' in various ODL institutions.
- Link to all the related ODL institutional digital repositories.
- Expertise available in various ODL institutions etc.

Digital libraries of ODL institutions should aim at providing the following services to the learners:

- Digital/virtual reference service.
- Information service through e-mail.
- Access to OPACs.
- Powerful search tools to retrieve the whole or parts of a digital documents, etc.

Apart from providing wider access and free flow of information to distance learners and to all those involved in open distance education, the proposed digital library provides several advantages. Some of these are:

- Networking and sharing of resources can be done easily.
- It provides cost effective solutions to libraries.
- More information can be provided at the press of a button. The user do not have to travel from long distances and his/her time and resources will be saved.
- Information can be updated continuously much more easily.
- Collaboration and exchange of ideas is possible.
- Improved preservation of resources.

So far, the Indian digital library initiatives are mainly seen as academic and research oriented. Though some useful resource material such as land records, cartographs, policy documents, legal judgments, parliamentary discussions etc., are being made available, they are not on large scale. Most of these initiatives are done in isolation without any coordination with other similar institutions. It can also be seen that many of the initiatives are one time projects with a limited grant, often without any proper planning for continuity. Important issues such as project objectives, preservation methods, content selection, coordination with other similar initiatives, access mechanism, sustainability and cost factor are not addressed.

9

Quality Assurance in Distance Learning

The open and distance learning in India owes its origin to the policy thrusts seeking answers to the question of quality education for large populations that remain outside the university system. The recommendations of a seminar organised in 1970 jointly by the University Grants Commission and the Ministry of Information and Broadcasting to discuss the related issues led to the constitution of a working group to study the concept and the utility of open distance education. The group strongly recommended the establishment of a national open university by an Act of Parliament in 1975.

Now there are 12 state open universities and one National Institute of Open Schooling (NIOS) in operation in India. In addition, there are over 100 institutes/centres of distance education (IODEs) in conventional central and state universities/ institutes. The number of programmes offered by the state open universities ranges from 3 at Netaji Subhash Open University, Kolkata, to 60 at Yashwantrao Chavan Maharashtra Open University (YCMOU), Nashik. The average annual growth of enrolment in IODEs has been about 9.5 per cent over the past few years now. All of them have identified their specific areas of intervention/specialisation for the benefit of their local clientele.

For example, YCMOU conducts programmes in home gardening, fruit production, vegetable production, floriculture and landscape gardening for practising farmers, farm labourers and the rural youth; Dr. B.R. Ambedkar Open University, Hyderabad, offers programmes in mushroom cultivation; the U.P. Rajarishi Tandon Open University, Allahabad, offers a programme in desktop publishing and at the NIOS, New Delhi, vocational education is being offered alongside the formal academic courses. The areas addressed under the vocational education programme at the school level by the NIOS include engineering and technology, agriculture, business and commerce, home science, health and paramedical studies and computer applications. IGNOU has been making pioneering efforts in offering courses in as many as 104 programme areas, covering a very wide range of subjects such as computing, nursing, management, creative writing, rural development, Panchayati Raj, disaster management, participatory forest management, tourism and women's empowerment.

In India, developments unique to open and distance learning system in the formal higher education include high enrolments, multimedia interventions, mainly in the form of audio-video materials, and live human support wherever necessary. It essentially seems to be a case of widening access to cover larger numbers, capitalising on the information age, reaching the unreached and offering quality programmes. A training programme using the distance mode of learning reaches large numbers and also helps avoid the physical dislocation of participants, provides flexibility and helps capitalise on information technology. Further, we witness that technology is not only improving but also becoming more accessible. Its use helps distance education applications become easier and more interactive. It not only reaches people across social, economic and geographical boundaries but also covers a very wide range of subjects. In addition, distance and open learning systems are also shaping as effective tools for catalysing development.

9.1. APPROACH TO QUALITY ASSURANCE IN ODL

Until recently, the terms quality and standards in education were not defined explicitly. It was possible to recognise quality without having to define it. However, traditionally, a few criteria have been used to designate institutions and/or their operations as either standard or sub-standard. First, the traditional benchmarks for a quality institution of higher education were adequate infrastructure and well-qualified and experienced faculty. Second, an institution was required to prescribe and ensure commonly recognised entrance standards and duration of studies for its various courses and programmes. Third, an institution needed to prescribe curricular content and an evaluation scheme for each course/programme. Last, it required a prescribed scheme for the educational transaction (such as x number of lectures, y number of tutorials, z number of practicals, etc.) to complete a course/programme successfully. All this ensured that the institution was imparting education of a good standard. This has been and generally continues to be the convention in face-to-face education.

Against these criteria, when the question of standards came up in relation to open distance education during the late 1960s and the 1970s, a new set of additional criteria was identified to reflect quality in them. The first and the most significant of these was, and continues to be, the process of course preparation together with the quality of the study materials thus prepared. The second concern was the provision made for the learning/teaching transaction, which incorporated feedback and interactivity in the guise of counselling, tutorials, assignments, etc. The third important concern was the usability of ODL for the subject concerned (for example, notwithstanding the innovation of experimental kits sent to the learner's home, ODL was considered unsuitable for teaching sciences in many parts of the world). These criteria formed the backbone of quality assurance in ODL from its very inception.

The major uneasy difference between the two systems lay in their different and differing transactions—the extent of contact between the teacher and the taught as well as the levels of socialisation, sharing of experiences and visible involvement in the process of learning. Today, however, there is a view that the importance of interaction is overrated; and therefore, it is enough to maintain balance between the content and interaction, of which the quality rather than the quantity should concern us. The other cause of uneasiness is the flexible entrance qualifications provision, which demonstrates that, in the case of open systems, exit behaviour has precedence over entry requirements. Many face-to-face institutions are highly selective and enrol the best students, an input measure often not available to ODL institutions operating on principles of open access. This uneasiness continues to accompany ODL operations, in differing measures, in the developing world even today.

By the 1980s, ODL theoreticians and practitioners, while giving due credence to reasonable quality concerns and criteria as espoused within conventional norms, had enriched their experience with ODL and thus mustered enough courage to discard earlier inhibitions and become more definitive about the components of quality assurance patently specific to ODL.

Process-based systemic concerns: The processes that came to be assessed and evaluated are those of curriculum design; course preparation including instructional design, developmental testing and peer review; assignment handling and turnaround time for feedback; course delivery including student support services; student evaluation and programme evaluation; and overall monitoring of the entire system, including its costefficiency and effectiveness. The conclusions drawn from such an assessment came to be used for improving the existing processes progressively. The link between the assessment and the corresponding improvement became cyclic, consequent upon which the system improved with every passing year.

Values-based philosophical concerns: On the social plank, one of the major arguments for ODL has been its ability to increase access to education together with facilitating equity in an area which has all along been a preserve for the elite. Questions such as "Is the ODL programme under consideration reasonably sensitive to these social concerns?" became critical in rating the strengths of a programme. Yet another question came up with the changing social, political and economic environment all over the world, as the changing needs and expectations of learners highlighted the arrival of the *new learner* questioning the relevance of many a traditional course. Are ODL programmes socially relevant; do they meet the needs and expectations of the new learners? As a new system, has ODL impacted the educational system in any significant way, and so, too, the social and economic systems? ODL operations came to be assessed against these questions and their quality rated accordingly.

Transaction-based pedagogic/androgogic concerns: All educational and training transactions (inputs-outputs) pertain to diverse combinations of cognitive, psychomotor and affective elements. Transactions in ODL operations too came to be assessed in terms of these very elements (thereby assigning still higher quality value to curriculum construction and instructional design in ODL), but not necessarily using the same norms and techniques as are well established in the face-to-face system. For example, in ODL systems, question papers may be derived from question banks, on-demand examinations may be a norm, some of the experiments may be conducted at home, and no two students may have the same value for all the tutorials provided.

As you can see from the above outline of the three major concerns, quality in ODL came to be measured on the basis of criteria, which go beyond those of qualified and experienced faculty and/or infrastructure. In addition to these developments, growing concerns about the funding-accreditation links in higher education prompted many developed countries to come up with quality assurance protocols addressing both the conventional and the distance learning modes. Many of them appeared in the 1990s, thus making it the decade of quality assurance. Consequently, internal and external assessments of the products and processes gained currency as a standard quality assurance strategy.

These practices and their outcomes, however, were being overtaken by events almost simultaneously, though more visibly during the 1990s, as e-Learning entered the field with multimedia packages and the allied high-tech possibilities. Towards the end of the last century, work began on learning objects and instructional management systems. Corresponding to these latest developments, the first five years of the present decade have seen developed countries making rapid strides in educational technology and working out new directions for their quality assurance mechanisms, but by and large most of the institutions in the developing world are yet to harness the new possibilities created by repositories of learning objects and instructional management systems.

The industrial and market orientation for the assessment of educational enterprise seemingly helped in reducing the popular prejudice against ODL, as both the face-to-face and distance modes of education began to be scrutinised and assessed in one and the same way. In many developed countries in the West, where an accredited ODL course is as good as an accredited face-to-face course, the mode of education has ceased to be a deciding factor in judging its standards as well as quality. What matters is what is done under each mode. In particular, the quality of the transaction is seen reflected in the products, the processes and now also the outcomes (levels of learners' learning, competence and satisfaction, employability of graduates vis-à-vis the perceptions of employers and the long-term socio-educational impact) of a system, rather than in the system (or its nomenclature) itself. Most of the developing world, however, continues to labour under the burden of tradition.

9.2. ODL QUALITY ASSURANCE PROGRAMMES

9.2.1. ODL in Non-formal Sector: An IGNOU Project

The realisation that ODL applications can help in achieving the developmental objectives sets an agenda for ODL that is different from its applications in higher education. The non-formal and adult education programmes, offered through the conventional systems in India, typically emphasise the acquisition of basic literacy and numeracy skills. In recent years, however, it has been recognised that these programmes must be integrated with a variety of development objectives that enable learners to apply their skills in the process of lifelong learning. The Fifth International Conference on Adult Education held in Hamburg in 1997, in defining adult education, stated that:

> "the objectives of Youth and Adult Education...are to develop the autonomy and the sense of responsibility of people and communities, to reinforce the capacity to deal with the transformations taking place in the economy, in culture and in society,...in short to enable

> people and communities to take control of their destiny and society...".

Besides, innovative methodologies that address the learners' aspirations for social, cultural and economic development are also being developed universally. Thus, there seems to be a strong reason for introducing and using distance and open learning methodologies as key components of any educational and training intervention required in rural India for integrated solutions to issues pertaining not only to access and equity, but also to development.

Providing an ever-widening access to growing numbers of individuals, particularly from disadvantaged groups, and ensuring the relevance of educational/ training programmes to the emerging needs and requirements of a fast-changing society is a colossal challenge in India. Among many of its kind, one such challenge was thrown up in 1993 when a historic amendment was made to the Indian Constitution to endow panchayats, the grass roots level democratic institutions, with the strength and prestige associated with the institutions of self-government so that they could play the desired significant role in determining the direction of development.

As a result of this amendment and the subsequent elections, over 3 million people, more than one-third of them women, were elected to various tiers of local self-government throughout the country. The absence of preparedness on the part of these key personnel, who would be the agents of change, was perceived as a major constraint in engineering the process of social transformation. Keeping in view its limited capacity, it was not possible for the conventional training system to face the challenge of training these millions of people's representatives.

Empowerment of the elected members of *panchayats* through appropriate awareness programmes therefore acquired the highest priority in the agenda for social action. The emerging potential of information and communication technologies was already pointing to appropriate and cost-effective means to meet this challenge through the distance mode of learning. Accordingly, a massive programme of education and training for these elected members was taken up as an independent project under a project directed by the Indira Gandhi National Open University (IGNOU) with the support of the Ministry of Rural Development, Government of India. The project that emerged is an attempt to sensitise the elected representatives to their roles and responsibilities in realising the socio-economic transformation of their communities and areas of residence.

The main objective of the programme is to empower the rural masses for their effective participation in the process of self-governance through their elected representatives in panchayats. With the determination to develop an exemplary quality programme for this non-formal sector, the project team decided on the strategy of integrating the following four distinct activities to achieve the objective.

9.2.1.1. ODL in Training Panchayati Raj Functionaries

The first task was to establish convincingly a case for using ODL methodologies in the training of Panchayati Raj functionaries. In India, in the rural development sector, there are more than 250 institutions that are directly or indirectly engaged in training in the various aspects of rural development and *Panchayati Raj*. These include:

- Those institutions and organisations which were either established by the central or state governments or are being funded fully or partially by the government. Some of them are also registered under the Registered Societies Act. Apart from three apex institutions, viz. Lalbahadur Shastri National Academy of Administration (Mussoorie), National Institute of Rural Development (Hyderabad) and the Indian Institute of Public Administration (New Delhi), other institutions placed in this category include state institutes of rural development (SIRDs), state administrative training institutions/academies and state Panchayati Raj training institutions.

- Those autonomous research and training institutions, which are engaged in related fields having bearing on the training efforts aimed at the Panchayati Raj elected functionaries. Their activities are funded by various agencies, including the government. They are mostly engaged in research and training.
- Those institutions that work as non-governmental organisations (NGOs), whose major functions are social action, social work/orientation and empowerment at grass roots level.

On average, a conventional training institution conducts about 40 to 50 training programmes of 1 to 3 weeks' duration per year, covering about 20 to 25 participants in each of these programmes. The physical output of each institution in terms of persons trained per year comes to about 1000 to 1200. If all these institutions, numbering about 250, were asked to do nothing but to conduct training for the elected members of the panchayats, it would take them about 12 years to complete one round of training to cover about 3.4 million elected functionaries. It was, therefore, necessary to look for alternative arrangements/mechanisms which could be applied as effective complementary training interventions for updating the knowledge and skills of the vast numbers of elected and other development functionaries. The distance mode of learning, with its multimedia approach, provides one such alternative to complement and reinforce the existing training arrangements. It was clear that there was no other way of going about the task at hand.

Pedagogical Soundness of Training

In order to achieve the overall goals of the project, it was considered essential that the elected representatives were equipped adequately with the knowledge and awareness about the concepts and practices of self-governance and also the skills necessary to shoulder the responsibilities of formulating and implementing developmental programmes. It was not an easy task, because the programme was to be addressed to a vastly heterogeneous rural population which consists of the educated, the neo-literate as well as the illiterate. They have differing learning styles and varied preferences. This necessitated the application of a sound pedagogical treatment to the content of training. An innovative multimedia approach to learning was therefore considered necessary. It was decided that the learning package to be developed should consist of self-learning print material (SLPM), an audio-video package and contact programmes for intensive counselling.

The SLPM was expected to cover a very wide range of subjects, ranging from the basic features of the Indian Constitution to themes like development with social justice. The process included the transformation of complicated technical programme manuals developed by the ministry for various rural development programmes into simple SLPM. The language and presentation of the

SLPM was, therefore, kept utterly simple. Initially it was thought that Michael West's *A General Service List of English Words* might be helpful in simplifying the language. What, however, worked was a combination of command over the language and the subject matter, and it was this approach that came to be instrumental in taking the task to its logical end.

In order to make the material, comprising 23 booklets in all, more interesting and relevant, it was illustrated extensively. Almost every page of the SLPM is illustrated. Illustrating study materials, however, is not only a time-consuming process, but also a difficult and challenging one. It calls for a sound knowledge of the subject matter and a full understanding of the context—the clientele and the environment. The very effective visual content of almost each page of the SLPM materialised through the use of graphic illustrations, which turned the SLPM into a form that could be accessed and assimilated even by the neo-literates.

Use of Media

The audio-video programmes accompanying the print material are intended to supplement the print material and help in the assimilation of the content. In addition, they add an interactive element to the package and are expected to help those deficient in study skills to optimise learning from the SLPM. This way, these programmes realise the creative potential and effectiveness of the medium. In essence, these audio-video programmes are integral to the learning strategies devised for the entire programme.

Media interventions, however, cannot be expected to achieve the desired results unless they are easily accessible to the target group. In the Indian rural situation, one cannot depend totally on the state-run television broadcasts to reach the masses everywhere. Lack of the necessary infrastructure constrains the process further.

Special arrangements were therefore made to enable the target beneficiaries to view programmes through a mobile reception system that was made available at *haat bazaars,* the weekly markets, normally held for marketing local products in rural areas. In one of the four districts, Dhar, covered in the initial phase, a 50-day campaign was drawn up for the dissemination of information through the presentation of the audio-video packages at 68 of these *haat bazaars* (weekly markets). Similarly, in another district, Bastar, which is otherwise inaccessible, audio-video packages were shown at 150 *haat bazaars*. These presentations attracted considerable attention from the target clientele and the feedback received was quite encouraging.

Contact-based Counselling

Initially, the SLPM and audio-video programmes were introduced in just one state, namely Madhya Pradesh, having 58,000 elected members of the local self-government. The size and the wide geographical dispersion of the clientele group, together with the divergent learning styles and preferences of its members, necessitated additional learner support in the form of contact programmes for intensive counselling to clarify any doubts which might arise during the process of learning from the materials. The creation of a cadre of local counsellors was a part of the training strategy designed for this purpose. Accordingly, a cadre of 350 local counsellors was trained with the help of master trainers. These local counsellors have since then conducted hundreds of counselling sessions at grassroots level.

Strategy for training the counsellors: The strategy for creating a cadre of local counsellors included, among other elements, a training programme to prepare master trainers identified by the state government concerned and drawn from the four selected districts. This first-step-training programme aimed at building up the knowledge and skills of the selected potential trainers in the pedagogy as required and the role of counselling in distance learning systems. Since the end product was expected to be a cadre of master trainers well equipped with the pedagogical skills that would enable them to train local counsellors, the following major areas were given special attention in this programme:

- A knowledge component, familiarising them with the panchayat, the local self-government system.
- An understanding component, covering the why and how of distance learning and the role of electronic media in its dispensation.
- A skills component, covering the necessary skills required of a counsellor in distance learning systems.
- An attitude component, including a positive disposition towards the need for capacity-building among elected local self-government members/ functionaries.

The process of training was not only participatory, but also included demonstrations of the skills required of an effective counsellor. Role-playing played an important part in imparting the necessary skills to the participants. The details of the master trainers' training programme were recorded as a manual for the trainers to help them when they conducted their respective training programmes. This proved to be a very useful tool for the second stage of training—that of local counsellors.

The integration of the text with the corresponding illustrations, highly effective media inputs and local counselling made the material so interesting and the programme effective enough to qualify for and earn the Commonwealth of Learning President's Award of Excellence in March 1999.

9.2.2. Quality Assurance Initiatives in YCMOU

Established in July 1989, the Yashwantrao Chavan Maharashtra Open University (YCMOU) was the fifth open university in India, a country that has 12 open universities today apart from a large number of distance education institutions. Maharashtra, the second most populated state in India, has a rich tradition of social and educational reform.

Registering approximately 125,000 learners annually for a wide variety of academic programmes spanning the full range from certificate to post-graduate and the research level, YCMOU already has a cumulative enrolment of 932,500 learners. These learners are catered to by an extensive network of eight Regional Centres, some District Centres, and over 2,000 Study Centres. The self-instructional material, developed for the 685 courses included in the 82 academic programmes on offer, runs into 1,271 course books, 342 videos, 311 audios and a large number of CD-ROM modules. The learner profile reflects a large number of employed persons from diverse vocations, housewives, persons from rural and tribal areas and also from the disadvantaged sections of society apart from some senior citizens, a few of them in their seventies. While catering to the needs of the common man, the university has also kept pace with the latest technological advances, especially those in information and communication technology. Today, with an experience of just about 16 years, the university has already established a name for itself, not only at the state and national levels, but also at the international level through the receipt of the COL Award for Institutional Excellence in Distance Education in the year 2002.

It is comparatively easy to describe factual developments in an ODL institution. It is much more difficult to make judgements about their quality. Besides, quality being a rather subjective, contextual matter, it may be examined from different analytical perspectives, varying as per the needs of the different stakeholders in the system. Thus, for the learner as the primary stakeholder, quality covers the entire gamut of a university's functions; for the government, the terms quality and best practice probably refer to the most cost-effective operations/products; for the academic community, it may be viewed in terms of knowledge gains; from the employer's point of view, the suitability of the product for commercial gains may be the yardstick and for the education providers, it may mean something that attracts learners and ensures social acceptability for what they offer.

Although YCMOU has not spelt out specific quality parameters, experience rather than theorisation has dominated the scene. The term best practice in the context of YCMOU refers to an initiative that is taken after considerable deliberation, is off the beaten track, has been introduced because of an emerging social need, has stood the test of time for a wide spectrum of learners and even though perhaps not systematically documented, has meant a value addition. It is in this light that the *best practices* of the university are considered here. For purposes of convenience, they have been grouped as follows:

— Institutional commitment and support.

— Curricular flexibility.

– Flexibility in learning strategies.
– Learner support.
– Assessment and evaluation.

9.2.2.1. Institutional Commitment and Support

Institutional commitment has been witnessed from different points of view: sensitivity to the needs of the learners, sustained efforts at developing relevant academic programmes, a concern for creating a trained and qualified workforce, a focus on upgrading resources to cope with advances in technology, a strong orientation towards systemic research and an openness towards objective appraisal of institutional practices—all this with the affirmed purpose of becoming a "mass varsity."

Sensitivity to the needs of learners has been shown in a variety of ways, especially through an insistence on prompt and accurate communication regarding relevant matters. Furthermore, all-round personality development of the learners has been supported through actively helping students to participate in the inter-university sports events and youth festivals generally organised for university students. Special concern has also been shown for the visually challenged through specially designed courses in computer science. A very unique initiative conveying an institutional commitment to a neglected section of society has been the provision of free education facilities to inmates of prisons at two places in Maharashtra. Many of these learners have now completed studies up to the first-degree level.

Programme development has been undertaken with due attention to the need for and relevance of a particular programme. The overriding concern at all times has been the needs of potential learners as well as consonance with the needs of the state and indirectly of the nation as a whole. Besides, the vocational potential of the programme from the viewpoint of the learners has also been emphasised.

Training of the entire staff—administrative, technical, professional and academic—in computer skills has been achieved with the result that almost every employee of the university is well versed in basic computer skills. Opportunities for professional development of the faculty and technical staff through externally conducted training programmes are also provided regularly.

Upgrading of infrastructure has been undertaken periodically through procuring the latest computer hardware and software, in-house development of various types of application software as well as the outsourced development of comprehensive software on the latest dotnet platform for systematising all the university's academic and administrative operations, right from registration to final certification. This software, though presently in its pilot-testing phase, offers an integrated view of the university functions while at the same time allowing for parametric control in the design of each academic programme. The dotnet platform, with its inbuilt security features, permits general and Web-based access to authorised functionaries only. Augmentation of infrastructure in terms of buildings, equipment, etc., to keep pace with the developmental plans of the university, is also a regular feature. The lush green and beautiful university campus houses separate buildings for important university functions like examinations, general administration, academic programme development, audio-visual production, etc. The university personnel, an important component of the overall resource base, are recruited through a comprehensive procedure to ensure that the most capable and qualified hands are employed. A regularly adopted employee performance appraisal system further ensures steady performance.

A major challenge to an educational system geared primarily towards mass education, is the development of a strong research base. YCMOU was the first open university in the country to offer academic programmes at the post-graduate and research level. "Communication" has been identified as the core research area and an emphasis has been placed on systemic research. A rather novel practice is that the research students are required to make three mandatory research presentations before a "research panel" prior to submitting their dissertations.

Openness towards objective appraisal of institutional practices has been evidenced through the assessment and accreditation voluntarily sought from the National Assessment and Accreditation Council (NAAC). Behind this step has been YCMOU's strong commitment to quality.

9.2.2.2. *Curricular Flexibility*

Flexibility in curricular offerings has been introduced both in order to maintain the spirit of "openness" as well as to provide for "cultural contextualisation" so that the learning materials become appealing to diverse users. Modularity as recommended in "Course Development Best Practices" (2002–2004) has been introduced in all the academic offerings so as to maintain coherence in course content within a given module and allow for learner mobility.

While due attention has been paid to elaborate procedures of instructional design and material development, a very distinctive feature of this university has been the wide range of curricula being handled. The spectrum covers the lowest level of skill-based, certificate programmes for those who have had very few years of formal education all the way up to the highest level of research-based programmes leading ultimately to an M.Phil. or a Ph.D. degree.

Agricultural education has been an important focus for this university in view of the large rural population of the state. Apart from the mass education programmes dealing with agriculture, computer literacy, development of self-help groups for teaching pre-primary level children, etc., there are a number of professional programmes in the field of teacher education, library science, management science, journalism and the like; programmes of a technological nature; and various Continuing Education programmes involving technical or vocational skills like lathe operation, masonry, interior designing, fashion designing, beauty parlour management, etc. Now, in response to some important social needs, programmes are being developed in the areas of health science, human rights and co-operative management too. Another rather unique contribution that addresses the needs of distance learners has been the programme on self-learning skills.

In addition to developing programmes that are relevant, periodic enrichment and updating is undertaken through new additional modules. Major programme re-structuring exercises have also been completed. For instance, the inclusion of courses and units like "General Knowledge and Social Awareness," "Marital Adjustment," "Rural Sociology," "Environment and Pollution," "Consumer Protection," "Office Services," "Personality Development," etc., under the Bachelor's Degree programme have made the programme both multi-disciplinary as well as applied in nature. Similar initiatives have been seen for programmes in Agriculture, Management Science and also the Teacher Education programmes through the "diagnostic approach to micro-teaching" introduced here.

9.2.2.3. Flexibility in Learning Strategies

The real issues with respect to appropriate learning strategies are not technical but curriculum-driven and pedagogical. It is well recognised that distance education courses should be able to accommodate a variety of learning styles and strategies—visual, auditory and kinesthetic. There is, therefore, the responsibility for providing a variety of learning resources (print, video, CD-ROM, WWW, etc.).

The learning strategies selected by learners are probably based on their cognitive profiles. These cognitive profiles can range from intellectual-minded persons, at ease with theorisation and abstractions, to the pragmatic and application-driven students, who prefer to deal with concrete situations. Thus some learners may be naturally more autonomous and creative so that they feel at ease with innovative approaches, with alternative options, and even with the challenge of trying to construct knowledge themselves. Others may prefer a solid and sure approach and a clear and straight content. Fortunately, with the current developments in ICT and particularly Web technology, offering a variety of options to the learners has become relatively easy. Despite this, with an increasing number of courses offered online and degrees offered through the Internet, quality concerns with respect to online education are coming to the forefront.

YCMOU has moved ahead steadily but cautiously with regard to learning strategies. The nature of course content and the technological readiness of the learner groups have largely determined the teaching–learning strategy adopted. While face-to-face counselling, enriched by differing proportions of the audio and video components, has been used in the theoretically oriented liberal education courses, hands-on practical experience has been provided in field and lab-based courses as in agricultural science, electronics engineering and the like. A rather innovative peer-learning approach called Prayog Pariwar has been introduced in agricultural courses. This involves the formation of self-help groups of practising farmers, each having a leader who is a student of this university and who is the direct agent for transmission of knowledge. Another paired peer-learning approach is seen through the operation of the coaching teams in the teacher education programme for effecting transfer of teaching skills among learners.

Extensive use of the latest Web-based communication technologies is seen in the engineering and computer programmes through the establishment of course-wise discussion forums, online counselling and feedback centres and the development of several virtual classroom modules (VCMs) "to create the supportive and cognitively stimulating environment so critical to effective learning". Besides, in order to get the feel of the real, the development of video-based animations and simulated digital practicals for the electronics courses are well underway.

9.2.2.4. Learner Support

In order to provide the resources and necessary support for the academic success of learners, YCMOU has established an extensive network of conveniently located Study Centres that are served by appropriately qualified and trained staff. The accompanying issues of equity and access have also been dealt with by adopting a sound rationale. A distinction has been made between the higher-end, professional programmes and the ones designed for mass education.

By and large, for professional programmes the university has established one Study Centre for each district in the state, whereas for the mass education programmes, the university has gone down to grass roots level at remote locations. The establishment of these remote location Study Centres for the low-end programmes has ensured that students are not required to travel a distance of more than 10 kilometres to access learning.

Special care has been taken to disseminate accurate and timely information about the institution, its programmes, courses, costs, related policies and requirements, etc., through the programme-wise prospectuses as well as a number of publications. Publicity through TV, radio and the mass media has helped potential learners to discover the curricular offerings, and pre-admission counselling on a one-to-one basis has helped them in making appropriate choices. Focused attention has been given to providing accurate and timely information to students opting for online registration, as in the case of the B.Tech. or Engineering programmes. These and similar programmes offering web-based support also handle the helpdesk function and provide information about redressing grievances, if required. Learner-friendly features are included in the course material before bulk production, but care is taken to see that the material reaches the student in time through an elaborately worked-out material despatch procedure. Although admittedly, the first despatch cannot take care of all the individual problems that surface later, backup arrangements for a second and occasionally a third round of despatches are in place.

Considering that "many students experience financial difficulties in accessing learning through distance learning systems and that a caring university must put financial aid packages in place", the university has made provision for fee concessions and partial freeships for deserving students from the underprivileged sector. A recent illustration is the South Asia Foundation (SAF) Madanjeet Singh Scholarship extended to 1197 students of YCMOU for pursuing post-graduate and vocational studies.

Realising that merely attracting learners to the system is not enough, the university has undertaken initiatives for providing sustained academic as well as administrative support to retain them in the system. The use of a TV channel during a given time-slot, the conduct of an interactive radio-counselling session once every month, the programme-wise academic inputs and administrative information given through the house journal called Samvad ("dialogue") and the recent use of the satellite-based communication system (EduSat) with technical support from the Indian Space Research Organisation are concrete initiatives taken in this direction. Under the EduSat facility, several Virtual Learning Centres have been commissioned in remote locations within the state, and the special type of interactive learning environment provided to the learners enables them to learn from the "best experts" in the field.

9.2.2.5. Assessment and Evaluation

In the context of learner evaluation, the YCMOU has developed a systematic approach for ensuring objective and reliable assessment of student learning. The continuous assessment component, that is normally viewed as necessary but difficult to implement in a distance learning set-up, has been implemented successfully in a number of academic programmes. With the accumulation of experience, however, periodic changes have been introduced to this component, mostly in terms of the weight assigned to it in the overall assessment of students as well as in the nature of evaluation tools that are being used currently.

The use of scientifically developed question banks as resource material for test construction has ensured reliable and valid tools of assessment. The question-wise synoptic answers and marking schemes supplied to examiners in a Central Assessment Programme have resulted in considerable objectivity in the assessment of student answer scripts and the mechanised process used for objective type questions involving hand-scoring stencils or the ICR technology has ensured both speed as well accuracy in assessment. The voluminous task of result processing has been handled effectively through a well-functioning computerised system that assists in giving quick and timely feedback to the learners.

Due attention has been paid to exercising controls at the stage of conducting examinations through careful selection and orientation of exam personnel. Problems or unfair practices brought to attention are promptly sorted through well-defined procedures. Some innovative steps in student evaluation have also been initiated. For instance, the Online Self Test Centre introduced for the Electronics Engineering Programmes provides unlimited Webbased opportunities for self-testing with immediate feedback on performance. A practice being introduced in the teacher education programmes involves giving students assignments based on the audios and videos prepared for them so that they may view their instructional material in an integrated manner. Application-oriented questions rather than those involving mere recall of facts and also principles have been introduced in some of the curricular offerings in an attempt to move gradually but certainly towards open-book type examinations. Considerable pilot work for offering on-demand and online examinations on a sustained basis is also well underway.

9.2.2.6. Impact of Quality Assurance Initiatives

Quality assurance has been viewed by this university as an ongoing endeavour with possibilities always available for improvement. It is this basic premise that has led the university to keep on experimenting, trying out new solutions to old problems and later reviewing these. The practices of the university stated here are, therefore, those that have had a long-term positive impact on the organisation. Below is a summary of the gains experienced both at the individual as well as the institutional level:

1. An overall sensitivity to the needs of the learner has been created at all levels in the organisation primarily because of the institutional thrust toward providing prompt services, especially considering the diverse backgrounds of the learners. Viewing the learner as a "whole person" is also an allied outcome resulting from an institutional concern for catering to overall personality development.
2. The focus on the development of needs-based academic programmes with flexibility to revise and add newer, more relevant course modules has sensitised the university faculty to the dynamic role expected of them.
3. The impetus given to staff training and professional development has resulted in improved efficiency at work, despite a small workforce.
4. The heavy use of computerisation in regular working has added both accuracy as well as speed to day-to-day operations.
5. The efforts at carrying education to prison inmates have given even the hard-core criminals, sentenced to life imprisonment, a constructive approach to life. As an important service rendered to those

abandoned by society, this has won much social accolade at the institutional level.

6. The peer-learning models evolved, the virtual classroom modules developed as learning resources and the use of TV and radio counselling as well as Web/satellite based communication technologies have provided considerable exposure to the staff and faculty for becoming multi-skilled professionals.
7. The importance given to research and the mandatory research presentations expected of research students, apart from having a motivating influence on the students, have also helped in developing appreciable sensitivity to rigour in scientific research among the YCMOU faculty.
8. The initiatives taken with respect to the development of course-wise question banks have helped the institution in creating a credible system of learner assessment.

With the rapid advances in communication technologies, the exponential growth of higher education institutes and the drastically reduced public financing of higher education, quality issues will always be at the forefront, especially in the context of GATS. A very important lesson for all those engaged in imparting higher education, particularly distance education, is to continually examine our so-called best practices with the firm conviction that the best practice of today can perhaps become even better tomorrow. For this, prior extensive documentation may not be as important as the dictates of first-hand experience. This is the approach that YCMOU has followed and also gained from.

Ideally, an institution may be considered to possess a quality culture when the need to achieve better outputs becomes an internalised passion for each and every employee. This need must be so deeply ingrained in every individual that it should guide further activity regardless of the external setting—favourable or unfavourable. Creation of this kind of need to improve continually on past performance or to contribute in a more effective manner is, to my mind, the key ingredient in developing a culture of quality in an institution.

9.3. CONCERNS OF QUALITY ASSURANCE

Driven by ICTs, ODL has been and is changing its profile rapidly, but the change is not uniform. ODL is not one and the same operation everywhere, nor even at any two institutions in the same country. Quality assurance concerns, protocols and practices, therefore, appear to be context specific. It appears reasonable to look at quality assurance, especially in the context of quality as a culture, along three dimensions—the core dimension, the systemic dimension and the resource dimension. The core dimension pertains to those factors that were identified in the second generation ODL operations. Their quality constitutes the foundation of quality assurance, whatever the context or generation of ODL that we may consider. This dimension pertains to learner-centricity (pointing to the importance of learning, not teaching, as a quality measure) and capacity-building (training/preparing academics and administrators to manage that shift). For both, research is a pre-requisite.

1. These factors are course materials and instructional design, the teaching-learning transaction (including learner evaluation practices) and learner support services, and they stand out uniformly in almost all the cases presented here. In particular, the cases that fall within the framework of second-generation operations have associated their quality assurance practices with these very three factors.

2. Learner support services need to be based on a thorough understanding of learners' circumstance, their abilities and requirements. This leads us to consider research as an allied core factor. Dynamic research activities are required not only for ascertaining the ground realities in relation to learners, but also for identifying what is required for capacity-building, how a course on offer fares, what may improve reflexivity within the institution and many other issues that need to be understood and analysed before solutions are worked out.

he systemic dimension pertains to those factors that onstitute the system of ODL at the institutional as well s the national level. Their importance became obvious rogressively as we moved beyond the second generation DL operations. This *dimension* pertains to the initiation nd introduction of quality assurance mechanisms, nternal as well as external, the symbiotic relationship etween the two and the management of both the nechanisms and the relationship.

3. The state appears to be a major factor in the process of introducing, promoting and sustaining quality assurance regimes in ODL as well as any other type of dispensation in both the developed and the developing countries.
4. The second most significant systemic factor contributing to quality assurance processes is institutional leadership, especially in the initial stages, when the institution is being set up and also when a particular programme is being conceived and developed.
5. The third systemic factor is institutional commitment, which appears to be essentially a function of leadership. It manifests itself in the form of objects, practices and attitudes. The objects

we refer to are institutional mission statements, vision papers or simply institutional aims and objectives as well as quality assurance policies and procedures which provide a direction and a path for the workforce. Practices such as adherence to state legislation through institutional procedures and their meticulous implementation, careful staff selection, staff sensitisation and capacity-building programmes, delegation of powers and assignment of corresponding responsibility to field operatives making them own the products and processes, efficient monitoring systems and appreciation for talent, innovation and tangible outputs not only constitute in themselves but also promote a culture of quality. The required attitude is seen in zero tolerance for inertia, inefficiency and indifference. It takes time to build institutional commitment. The leadership needs to be imaginative, patient and persistent to forge it.

6. The fourth systemic factor is innovative management. ODL institutions are of many grains and hues—no single model of management can suit them all. But there appear to be a few basics that should define their contours fairly clearly. Flexibility for making rational compromises and decentralising programme management, pragmatism for integrating sub-systems (especially in dual-mode institutions) and employing variable technologies for cost-efficiency and operational effectiveness, sagacity for promoting inclusive democratic and participatory management and/or isolating sick components for their overhaul, foresight for perceiving promising innovations, and integrity for eliminating distractions and negative forces are some of the features required of every ODL management unit.

7. The fifth systemic factor is the quality of long- as well as short-term planning and the execution of plans. Meticulous plans coupled with pragmatic execution contribute to the quality of products, processes and outcomes. Both the plans and the execution strategies must allow room for variations in relation to risks and the needed process modifications.
8. The existence of quality-assurance mechanisms that are integrated into institutional processes is the sixth systemic factor that we consider here. One such mechanism could be a quality assurance unit responsible for the related protocols. Other mechanisms with similar objectives could be in the form of institutional central units for ODL that, in part, take care of ODL quality assurance requirements.

The resource dimension has always been important, but with the advent of the fourth and the fifth generation ODL operations, the significance of resources has touched new heights. With its generic meaning, resources include technology, technical and academic expertise, learning resources and physical infrastructure. This *dimension* pertains to the pivotal factors that make changes and the management of changes possible and durable.

9. *Contemporary ICTs* have opened immense possibilities, but their availability is not uniform. Developed countries consider ICT applications and the related infrastructure a crucial factor in the process of ODL quality enhancement and show no hesitation in investing therein. Some other institutions are at different levels of development in this regard. What benefits they may reap and how is yet to be seen.

10. *The academic fraternity*, the soul of the enterprise, involved in ODL operations, needs to move out of the traditional garb and accept multiple responsibilities, especially those in dual-mode institutions, undergo training and retraining as new technologies come to aid educational dispensation, innovate to meet diverse learning needs and be ready to meet students at any time and anywhere through any technology.

9.4. TOWARDS A QUALITY CULTURE

The debate on and the quest for a quality culture in ODL will continue with the persistent rise in the social demand and value of education, developments in technology and epoch-making changes in educational thought—today, societies look up to education for economic development and quality of life, new technologies are creating digital natives with significantly different learning techniques, and the conventional experiential and constructivist ways of learning are questioned in view of the new learning paradigm of connectivism. Having scanned samples of contemporary quality assurance practices, we have been able to identify the crucial factors that promise the flowering of a quality culture.

The state is a major promoter of any cultural shift in educational dispensation. Progressive legislation, provision of adequate funding and monitoring have to be provided by the state. If the state is half-hearted in its approach to ODL, as is the case with some developing countries, the ODL system established will neither lead to nor constitute a culture of quality. This emphasis on state participation is clear from the OUUK, UoG and USQ cases. Governments need to revisit their policies pertaining to educational planning and financing, and put such policies in place as not only promote but also necessitate the creation of a quality culture in ODL. In addition, the telecommunications sector needs to be liberalised, and relevant enabling policies favouring ICT applications in ODL need to be put in place; for example, such applications may be subsidised in developing countries.

At the institutional level, leadership is the most significant engine of change, development and quality assurance. Leadership, especially at the initial stages of the development of an institution or a programme, has significant implications for a host of related micro-factors such as the quality of the overall management and that of the staff, their expertise and attitude.

(a) *Transparency* in operational and financial management lays the foundation of mutual trust among the components of the institution. The culture of such a trust allows honest and constructive criticism to flourish, which in turn creates a sense of belonging among all the cadres, as everything said and done is believed to be for the betterment of the institution and not seen to hurt or denigrate anybody.

(b) *Decentralisation* of both the formulation and the execution of policies promotes participatory management, which strengthens the sense of ownership among all the different levels of personnel for all that goes in the name of the institution.

(c) *Institutional commitment* is an aggregate of the commitments of those who make up the institution. Incompetent and unimaginative leadership cannot secure institutional commitment, even if it secures individuals' commitments on the basis of personal loyalty. Competent leadership does not depend on, nor look for, personal loyalty. It identifies staff strictly on the basis of the requirements of the institution; values, appreciates and acknowledges contributions, big as well as small, of all the members of staff; builds their confidence to make them proactive and helps them to reach their optimal levels of performance, leading to a culture of commitment so essential for quality assurance.

(d) *Proactive and innovative management,* necessitated by the present-day socio-educational dynamics, too, depends on the leadership. Creation of comfort zones for the workforce to perform optimally, seen as a panacea for institutional growth, does not appear to suit the dual deluge of demand for socially relevant education and the innovations in ICT applications across the globe and the rate at which these applications are woven with pedagogy. Invariably, ODL institutions find themselves in a continual state of crisis, making it necessary for the leadership not only to resolve the immediate crises, but also to be ever ready to face new ones as they tumble one upon the other continually. In ODL systems, therefore, policies have to feed crisis management, not comfort zones.

(e) To incorporate the above factors into institutional processes successfully, no leadership can depend entirely on introspection, textbook knowledge or borrowed research findings. Investments have to be made in institution-specific systemic research to inform institutional policies, practices and products.

(f) Investments have to be made in ICT applications as well. However daunting it may appear in the developing countries, the need for harnessing technology not only for institutional management, archiving and exchange of information and the management of students, pedagogy and student support services, but also for extending institutional reach beyond the state and national boundaries cannot be overemphasised.

(g) *Innovations* in policy frameworks, administrative processes, curricular and instructional design and technology applications have enhanced versatility and utility of ODL systems significantly. However, there are areas of concern which do not display any visible impact of innovations; for example, the content and the process of learner assessment has not changed in any appreciable measure—by and large, we continue testing learners for their memory and levels of information/ knowledge. Though curricular innovations emphasise the social relevance of ODL programmes and courses, there is hardly any corresponding development in the design of assessment tools to test learners' creativity, problem-solving skills or competence in the application of their learning. The broader the canvas of innovations, the brighter the prospects of quality assurance.

Above all institutional leadership must have a humane approach, for ODL deals with human beings as the basic raw material. It should put in place policies and mechanisms to take care of issues like human diversity, gender, etc. In this regard, it is worth speculating as to what may be the outcome of female leadership in ODL, as the task is essentially that of nurturing human beings. Unfortunately, at present there are not enough women in leadership roles in ODL to look for dependable inferences. Further, institutions need to revisit their missions and reorganise their operations, keeping in view the varied applications of technology, human resource requirements and market forces. Learners and educators need to be reoriented for the emerging technology-enhanced didactic transaction. This may require overhauling the existing systems of lower-level education as well. Overall, it appears that ODL management will be better off if it takes a corporate stance and the workforce, especially the academics, functions like a corporate community.

At the international, regional and national levels, cross-institutional collaboration is emerging as a meaningful driver of quality assurance initiatives and systems. The international systems will facilitate cross-border and trans-modal offerings, whereby not only will cross-cultural and multinational curricula find encouragement, but also capacity will be built among the partners equitably. Indeed international collaboration, including that in systemic research, promises not only to optimise resources by enlarging the scope and reach of the open educational resources movement, but also to facilitate diverse glimpses of quality and thus become the stimuli for raising the levels of products and services at all the institutions concerned.

Bibliography

Adalian, P. et al. (1997). "The student-centered electronic teaching library: A new model for learning". *Reference Service Review*, 25 (Fall/Winter), 11-21.

Amstutz, D. and Whitson, D. (1997). "University faculty and information literacy: who teaches the students?" *Research Strategies* 15, Winter, 18-25.

Aslam, M. (2000). "Education and Training for Millions: Pedagogical Challenges for Distance Education." *Open Learning 15, 3,* 309–315.

Association of College and Research Libraries. (1998). "ACRL guidelines for distance learning library services". *College & Research Libraries News*, 59(8), 689-694.

Bhattacharya, B. (2003). Country Paper on Improvements in Educational Productivity Promotion Through E-learning. *Presented in Asian Productivity* Organization sponsored seminar on "New Multimedia Strategies for Productivity.

Bruce, L. (2003). "The Standards Approach: Planning for Excellence in Distance Education." *Campus Technology*. Retrieved from www.campus-technology.com.

Campbell, T. et al. (2003). *Distance Education Best Practices Manual*. Retrieved from https://mycampus.phoenix.edu.

Covington, D., Petherbridge, D. & Warren, S. (2005). "Best Practices: A Triangulated Support Approach in Transitioning Faculty to Online Teaching." In *Online Journal of Distance Learning Administration VIII (1)*. Retrieved from http://www.westga. edu.

Floor P (2000): Networked Services for Quality Distance Learning, in *ODL Networking for Quality Learning,* in Proceedings of Lisbon 2000 Conference of the European ODL Liaison Committee, Lisbon.

Hülsmann, T. (2000) *The Costs of Open Learning: A Handbook.* Oldenburg: BIS, University of Oldenburg.

Jung, I. (2005). "Quality Assurance Survey of Mega-universities." In C. McIntosh and Z. Varoglu (Eds.) (2005). *Lifelong Learning and Distance Higher Education.* p.90. Vancouver: Commonwealth of Learning/UNESCO Publishing.

Koul, B. N. (2005). *Higher Distance/Virtual Education in the Anglophone Caribbean.* pp. 72–74. Caracas: International Institute for Higher Education in Latin America and the Caribbean (IESALC-UNESCO).

National Institute of Open Schooling, *Prospectus 2006-2007* (Academic Courses).

Perraton, H. (2000) *Open and Distance Learning in the Developing World.* London: Routledge.

Pillai, L. (2003). "Quality Assurance and Best Practices." In V.S. Prasad (Ed.) *Best Practices in Open and Distance Education.* pp. 51–68. Hyderabad (India): K. Ramakrishna Booklinks Corp.

Powar, K. et al. (2003). *Performance Indicators in Distance Higher Education.* New Delhi: Aravali Books International (P) Ltd..

Prasad, V.S. (2003). "Best Practices in Open and Distance Education: Problems & Concerns". In V.S. Prasad (Ed.) *Best Practices in Open and Distance Education.* pp. 1–5. Hyderabad (India): K. Ramakrishna Booklinks Corp.

Prensky, M. (2005). "The Future is Now: Strategies for Reaching Today's Students." A presentation made at the Western Cooperative for Educational Telecommunications (WCET) Conference at San Francisco, USA, in November 2005.

Russell, T. and McPherson, S. 2001 'Indicators of success in teacher education: a review and analysis of recent research' Paper presented to Pan-Canadian Education Research Agenda.

Tait, A. (2000): Planning Student Support in Open and Distance Learning, in *Open Learning,* 15 (3), 287-300.

Tulloch, J. & Sneed, J. R. (Eds.) (2000). *Quality Enhancing Practices in Distance Education: Teaching and Learning,* Washington, DC: Instructional Telecommunications Council. Retrieved from www.opencampus.com.

UNESCO (2000b): Analytical survey, *Distance Education for the Information Society, Policies, Pedagogy and Professional Development,* UNESCO Institute for Information Technologies in Education, Moscow: UNESCO/IITE.

Yang, Y. & Cormelious, L. (2005). "Preparing Instructors for Quality Online Instruction." *Online Journal of Distance Learning Administration. VIII (1).* Retrieved from http://www.westga.edu.

Index